"I'M SO GLAD TO BE ALIVE!

"I'm so glad to know that God created me in His own image, and while there may have been times when that image really got kinda loused up, I'm so glad that He *'has turned for me my mourning into dancing . . . and girded me with gladness.'* . . ."

God means love, and God's love means thankfulness on rocky places and smooth, during good times and bad, morning and night.

Mrs. Hunter knows—and here proves—that there is no occasion, no matter how trivial, no matter how bad, that does not serve some purpose in God's plan. And she knows that, no matter what happens, it is always right, always redeeming, to say:

PRAISE THE LORD ANYWAY!

P.T.L.A.

(Praise The Lord Anyway!)

Frances Gardner Hunter

1968

WARNER PRESS • **Anderson, Indiana**

P.T.L.A.
(Praise The Lord Anyway!)

A PORTAL BOOK
Published by Pyramid Publications for Warner Press, Inc.

Seventh printing April, 1973

Copyright © 1972 by Frances Gardner Hunter

All Rights Reserved

Printed in the United States of America

ISBN 0-87162-131-2

PORTAL BOOKS are published by Warner Press, Inc.
1200 East 5th Street, Anderson, Indiana 46011, U.S.A.

Contents

CHAPTER I

P.T.L. and P.T.L.A.
(Praise The Lord and Praise The Lord Anyway!)

Thou hast turned for me my mourning into dancing;
Thou hast loosened my sackcloth and girded
me with gladness,

THAT MY SOUL MAY PRAISE THEE AND
NOT BE SILENT,

OH LORD MY GOD, *I WILL GIVE
THANKS TO THEE FOR EVER.*

Ps. 30:11,12

DID YOU HEAR what God said to you in that verse? The first time I ever read that, it was as though it had been written just for me and no one else: "That my soul may praise Thee and not be silent, O Lord my God, I will give thanks to Thee for ever." What wonderful advice this is! Just praising God can lift you up into the very presence of God Himself. Now I don't mean uttering words that have no meaning or just repeating standard phrases, I mean honestly thanking God for all the good things in life.

The very love of God permeates my total being and knowing that God loves ME makes me want to shout from the housetops what He's done. We take so many things for granted in life, giving "coincidence" the credit instead of giving praise to God for what He has done.

I'm looking out the window right now as I sit at my desk and type and I can see so many things to give God thanks for. The sun is shining beautifully today and just the sunshine makes me think of the warmth of God's love. The brightness of the sun makes me realize so positively that Jesus is the light of the world. Just think what this world would be without sunshine. Can you imagine getting up day after day without sunshine?

7

Now in Texas not all days are sunny, and in your town not all days are sunny, but be honest now, don't the sunny days make it all worthwhile? And even if it were raining in Texas, I'd have to thank God for sending the cooling rains, the rains we need to keep our grass green, the rain we need to keep our reservoirs filled up so that we will have water to drink and for the necessities of life.

I look at the trees in my front yard and think of how many times, in countries all over the world, a traveler has found coolness and shelter under the shade of a tree. I look at the trees and think of how they are used to make the very paper this book is printed on. I look at the grass and think of how grass has fed the cows that give the milk that is processed and now sits in my refrigerator. I can see the flowers just starting to bloom, and I thank God for the beauty of even the tiniest little flower to make our life a thing of beauty.

Think seriously how God could have created the universe. He could have made it completely barren, with no trees, no vegetation, no birds to sing, no water to drink, no trees to find shelter under, and you know, He could have even made it without any people. And if He had made this entire earth without any people, I sure wouldn't be here, and so I thank Him for the very fact that He created people, even me!

I'm so glad to be alive! I'm so glad to know that God created me in His own image, and while there may have been times when that image really got kinda loused up, I'm so glad that He "hast turned for me my mourning into dancing; . . . hast loosed my sackcloth and girded me with gladness. . . ." So Lord I just want to thank You for creating me, for giving me a chance to be alive, for giving me the privilege of being a mother, for giving me the husband that You did.

Lord, I want to thank You for allowing me to accept myself as I am, and not wishing that I was someone else. Thank You, Lord for letting me accept myself as You see me, and not as I might see myself, because Lord if I saw myself in my own eyes, I might think I had a lot to complain about, but when I know that You love me just as I am, my heart jumps with joy and I'll thank You forever.

Why don't you take a piece of paper right now, and write down the things you could thank God for. And, you know, the most amazing thing will happen to you if you do this; you'll all of a sudden begin thinking of lots more things you can thank God for, and then before long you'll be amazed at what praising God will do to the things in life that we don't especially enjoy, or that we complain about all the time. If you spend your time saying "Praise the Lord," you won't have time to complain, and I never knew anyone who honestly felt better after complaining.

Whenever I go into a church, I always have the entire congregation give a big cheer with just the three words "Praise the Lord," and I'd like to tell you why. It takes people's minds off themselves and turns their eyes toward God. And in every church where I do this, the response is always the same. I usually remind them that Jesus Christ is the most exciting person in the world, and then ask them to all say "Praise the Lord." And you should hear the response. Most of the time they sound like they have a big stomach ache as they come out with a sick-sounding "Praise the Lord." It tickles me silly, because these same people at a baseball game, football game or basketball game would be yelling their heads off for something not nearly as important as God.

I always love to give a congregation a second chance because they become aware of how luke-warm they are about praising the Lord, and the second time the rafters really ring with those three words, "Praise the Lord."

Now it isn't what it does noise-wise that counts, it's what it does with the people concerned who really give

9

their lungs a workout on those three words. You can look around in any church, regardless of denomination, and there won't be a crab in the crowd when everyone has really enthusiastically complied with what the Bible says: "Let everything that breathes praise the Lord." There's a smile on the face of everyone present, because just taking the name of the Lord on your lips does something for you. Start trying it more often, will you? I guarantee it will do something for your spiritual growth.

Saying "Praise the Lord" can do a lot for you even if at that particular moment you can't think of any specific thing to be thankful for, but saying "Praise the Lord" when God really does something great is an even more exciting thing. But now . . . here comes the hardest part, and yet it should be one of the easiest parts. Can you say "Praise the Lord" when things don't go the way you want them to? Does your faith stay right up there when something turns out differently from the way you wanted it to? The Bible doesn't tell us to be thankful only for good things, but it tells us to be thankful for *all* things. I Thessalonians 5:18 (LNT) says: "Always be thankful *no matter what happens,* for that is God's will for you who belong to Christ Jesus."*

I'll never forget the first time someone said that to me. I thought he was nuts! My first comment was, "Even if I have a blowout?" I asked him that question because I had just had a blowout the night before and had walked about two miles to a gas station on the shoulders of the highway, which were not very easy to walk on, and my disposition had worn thin.

I was a brand-new Christian at the time, and this seemed to me to be about the silliest thing I could ever imagine, but when he backed up the statement with scripture, I began to wonder. He quoted Romans 8:28

The Living Bible, copyright 1971 by Tyndale House Publishers, Wheaton, Illinois 60187.

(LNT): "And we know that all that happens to us is working for our good if we love God and are fitting into His plans." I really took that verse to heart and began searching the Bible to see how this could possibly apply to life with all the things we are faced with today. I decided it had to be true, or it wouldn't be written in God's Holy Word. So I had no choice except to believe it, and begin to put it into practical experience.

Well, the Lord gave me an opportunity real fast. I had invited some friends over for dinner who were tremendous Christians, and I wanted everything to be absolutely perfect. Even though I was working, the night before I had made a super special dessert, and had gotten out all the silverware, polished it up beautifully, and was spending hours thinking of ways to make the dinner perfect.

I had a maid who was to put the meat in the oven at the prescribed hour and watch it carefully. Somehow or other, in my desire to have everything "perfect" I had forgotten to tell her what degree I wanted the oven turned to, and it had previously been set at 450 for biscuits the night before, so that's right where she left it. She put the meat on at the right hour, and with the temperature previously indicated. and by the time I got home from work, . . . you're right . . . the meat was singed beyond belief. As a matter of fact, it was so black on the outside it didn't even look like roast beef. I asked her if she had forgotten that I wanted her to watch it, and she said, "I watched it, and it sure got black, didn't it?"

Well, there it was—supper time, the guests drove up to the front door, fought their way through the smoke, and what to do? I remembered what this young man had said to me about giving thanks for all things, so I said, "Thank You Lord, for this beautiful dinner tonight which could be ruined by a burned roast." And do you know what happened? No longer was I concerned with whether or not the dinner was perfect, no longer was I concerned about what the guests thought, no longer was I feeling an urge to "bop" the maid on the head, but instead, just by saying those few little words, my eyes were immediately turned toward Christ, and the tension of the moment was gone forever. We all laughed as I explained the situation—we took the meat out of the oven, cut off the one-inch burned meat around all the edges, and sat down to enjoy the rest of the meal, with a fan blowing the smoke out of the house.

Before I became a Christian (or even after I became a Christian), had I not learned to give thanks for all things this particular night could have been one of the greatest defeats of my life and could have really been a nightmare. I could have been miserable, sick, ashamed, mad, furious—oh, I could have been any number of things—but just saying "thank you" in even the most adverse circumstances transformed the evening, because instantly when I said those words, our eyes turned toward Christ.

Many times we get our eyes on "things" other than Christ, and situations like this come up, to re-turn our eyes to Christ. As much as anything else, saying "Praise the Lord Anyway" relieves the tension of any situation. However, as with all of God's promises, there is a condition, and the condition in Romans is, "If we love God and are fitting into His plans."

The Bible doesn't promise that all things that happen to us will be for our good if we don't love God and if we aren't fitting into His plans, but it does promise this to those who love Him. This has gotten to be a regular, consistent part of my life, and as I relate many of the stories which will follow, you can see in each case, God took a negative situation and made a victory out of it.

Sometimes it takes great faith to believe that a miracle can come out of a disaster, but God is faithful if we will only believe. Saying, "Thank You, Lord, I don't know what for, but thank You anyway," can bring fresh consciousness of the reality of God and a fresh dependence upon the power of God, where otherwise we might be tempted to handle a situation on our own. It's easy to praise the Lord when things are good, but if you'll just try it when things look hopeless, I guarantee you it will really do something for your spiritual life.

Along about now, somebody is sure to be saying, "That's a Pollyanna theory, but it really doesn't work." Remember what Colossians 2:8 (LNT) says: "Don't let others spoil your faith and joy with their philosophies, their wrong and shallow answers built on men's thoughts and ideas, instead of on what Christ has said." Don't let ANYONE spoil your faith and joy. Look to God for the answer and see what happens. As long as our minds and thoughts are turned to Christ, it's fabulous what can happen to us. And even if you don't believe it, try it—what have you got to lose?

I remember a young man one time who prayed a prayer similar to this: "Lord, if You are real (and I don't think You are), I open the door of my life and invite You to come in and take control of my life." Today, because he was willing to discover for himself if God is real, he is one of the most outstanding Christians I know. You never know what might happen to you.

CHAPTER II

Praise the Lord for "No"

WELL, THERE IT HANGS— right in the center of the living room, just like God planned! But only did it become a reality after a P.T.L.A.—and this is how it all happened!

We recently redid our entire house—or I should say God's house, because it belongs to Him—and when it was nearing completion we had a huge vacancy right over the sofa where we needed a large painting. Charles and I had seen one painting that we wanted for our home, but the artist wouldn't sell it, since it was one of a series, and even though we had wanted to own it because it was such an outstanding picture, we said "Praise the Lord Anyway" when we got the letter advising us that it wasn't for sale. We gave thanks for all things, because we knew the Lord had something else in mind for us. Months went by and we still didn't know what God had for us instead of this particular painting, and then a series of "coincidences" began.

Charles and I had been praying that the Lord would send us the right painting for our living room and we had some real specifications. The living room is visible from the foyer as soon as you have entered the house, and we wanted a religious picture for this area so that as soon as someone came into the house, there would be no doubt in his mind that this was a Christian home. Unfortunately, many religious pictures are not particularly attractive, and we wanted one that would add to the decor of the house as well as portray the purpose of our home.

A woman in Houston read a copy of *God Is Fabulous,* and somehow or other it really communicated with her. She immediately went to the book store where she had bought it to ask how you would get in touch with an author. She felt it absolutely vital to talk to me personally. She explained to the book-store owner that the author lived in Miami, but wanted to know how you approached someone like this (she didn't realize just like you would anyone else). By "coincidence" the bookstore owner had a customer who had recently told him that the author of *God Is Fabulous* had married the man who was his C.P.A. The owner told the lady that I didn't happen to be Mrs. Gardner any longer, and I didn't happen to live in Miami any longer, but that I was recently married and living in Houston, Texas. By "coincidence" the book-store owner knew who to call to find out what my correct name was and how my husband would be listed in the phone book.

The reader along with two friends promptly got in her car and drove out to my house. They were so nervous they drove past the house five times before they finally got up enough courage to knock on the door. When they did, my daughter opened the door and then told them I was out of town, but that I would be back the next day and to please call me because I'd be delighted to hear from them. As soon as I got home I got a phone call asking me to speak at a home Bible-study group, and even though I was in the middle of a real hectic schedule and was preparing to leave home again within three days, the Lord told me to accept. And so I did, knowing full well that I was squeezed for time.

I went to the Bible-study group the next day, and as I walked into the house where it was being held, I noticed a painting of roses. Peculiarly, I'm not fond of pictures of just roses, but for some reason or other, I saw something that I really liked about this picture, so I commented on it because it really caught my eye. We had an exciting time at the Bible-study group and when it was over and I left, I commented again on the beautiful roses, and I couldn't understand this, because I don't like paintings of flowers! But God knew.

The next day I got a phone call from two of the girls who were at the Bible study and they wanted to know if I could take time out for a little counseling, and even though I was really jammed up for time, since I was leaving town the next day, somehow or other, God's green light said to tell them to come ahead.

They came out to the house, and after talking with them a while, I made a comment about the picture I had seen the day before. They said, "Our Sunday-School teacher painted that, didn't you know that?" I said that I didn't. They looked at the house and then I explained about the blank space on the wall, and explained that we were asking God to lead us to the right picture for the space, and one of the girls said, "Did you know the lady who painted the roses paints beautiful religious pictures?" I said, "She does?" And after a few minutes' conversation, the other girl said, "Would you like to go out and see her paintings after you come back from your trip?" I said, "No, I'd like to go right now!"

My husband was working at home this particular day and when he heard me say this, he knew the strain I was under to complete all the correspondence I had, etc., so he came out and said, "Honey, don't you think you ought to wait until you come back?" I turned to him and said what was in my heart. "Charles," I said, "I feel led to go today!" Charles didn't say another word, because he knew that God had spoken to me, so he just patted me and said, "Go ahead, honey!" The girls had to return to where their children were, pick them up out of nursery school, get a baby sitter and return to my house, which is exactly what they did, and we went out to see the artist.

She had many beautiful paintings in various stages of completion which I greatly admired, and as we shared the excitement of Christ, our spirits really blended together and she began to talk to me about what type of painting I wanted. The other girl mentioned that the artist had painted a beautiful Garden of Gethsemane, but had poured her heart and soul into it so much that she said she would never sell it or paint another one.

One time a famous evangelist saw it, and broke into tears because God's Holy Spirit communicated to him through it so vividly. Many many people had offered to buy it previously, but she had always rejected their offers, and many had asked her since to paint another one, but she always said "No" because it had drained too much out of her, and all of a sudden she said, "May I paint for you a special Garden of Gethsemane!"

I couldn't believe my ears. God's Holy Spirit had so enveloped all of us that I was overcome with tears. We made a date for her to come over to my house to see what the house looked like so that she could paint the picture that was just right for me. I couldn't wait to return from my next trip so she could come out to my house so I could really feel things were under way.

The day after I got back from my trip, Mildred came over. She looked at our living room, and Charles and I shared with her our feelings about Christ and how we felt Christ must have looked. Rugged, but gentle; manly, but loving; masculine, but compassionate; strong, but understanding of weakness; not wanting to be crucified, but willing to be obedient. We were all so excited about what God had done in bringing us together, we formed a prayer circle and asked God to paint upon the artist's mind exactly the picture He wanted for our house. Spiritual goose pimples covered all of us as God's Holy Spirit became so strong at that moment, evidence that He was behind all of this.

Mildred went home and feverishly began to paint day and night, night and day. She said she had never been so inspired in her entire life—and then it was finished! She called me to bring it over—I called my husband to come home from the office and then it was here. The picture we had prayed so much for—the picture we had prayed so much about—and we were about to see what God had painted on Mildred's mind. As I was waiting for my husband to arrive, I really felt like I was having a baby, I was so wound up.

Finally Charles got there—and we all prayed and thanked God for painting it—and then the wrapping was removed! We cried! The most beautiful eyes of Jesus I have ever seen looked at me and said, "May I serve in your home?" My heart said, "No, no, no, no, you may have the whole house, not just be a servant,"

17

and He said back softly, "I came that YOU might have life, and have it abundantly."

We looked at the picture and cried off and on the entire day long. After supper that night, for the first time in our marriage, we didn't get right up and do the dishes —we went into the living room, turned the light on over the painting, and sat and read the story of the Garden of Gethsemane in each of the gospels. As we read the details, we found faintly in the background the entire story—the City of Jerusalem a half-mile away—the disciples sacked out below Jesus—the whole story, just like it occurred two thousand years ago.

Looking back, I could have been very disappointed when I didn't get the original painting I wanted, but at the time we got the letter refusing to sell us the picture, Charles and I said: "P.T.L.A. Guess the Lord didn't want us to have it for some reason." We gave thanks because He didn't let us have it because we knew somewhere along the line we'd find out what He had planned for us, and we knew it would be best for us, so we didn't question Him, but only waited for what *He* wanted to give us.

People have said to us, "You can really tell it was made for the room, because it picks up all the colors in the furniture," but I say, "No, the room was made just for the picture, even though we didn't know it at the time!"

CHAPTER III

Praise the Lord for Football, Too!

I'M ALWAYS EXCITED about Jesus Christ, because He certainly is the most exciting man that ever lived, and I find it impossible to keep my mouth shut, since the old-timers like Peter, John, James, Paul, etc., went all over the place sharing the good news.

On one of my tours I was scheduled to go first to Tulsa, Oklahoma. One of my usual tricks is to never allow enough time to get to the airport, because I'm always so involved with so many things, but somehow or other I always manage to get on the plane with a few seconds to spare, and then just as I sit down I remember my luggage, and pray a quick prayer: "Lord, see that my luggage gets on the plane or I'll be singing 'Just as I Am' the whole trip"—and then I look out the window and the belly of the plane opens up and I see my luggage going on, so I relax and look forward to an exciting trip.

However, after rushing madly to gates too many times, I finally decided, on this particular trip, that I would take enough time and walk to the gate, because if I didn't I might have a heart attack some one of these days. So, I got to the airport about twenty minutes early and I sauntered leisurely up to the counter to present my ticket, and when I did, the clerk asked, "How are you going to get your luggage there?" I replied, "On the plane." He said, "How are you going to do that?" And I said, "Well, I've got a ticket!" But he said, "You're too late—it won't get on this plane."

I was really shocked, because it was the first time I had ever gotten to the airport this early and here was a clerk I surmised must have had a fight with his wife that morning, because he was in such a bad mood he insisted my bags wouldn't get on the flight.

I guess I surprised him because I just calmly said, "Well, put them on the next plane, then, if there isn't time to catch this one." I think he was real disappointed because he expected me to put up the usual fight and scream and yell because the bags weren't going to make it, but somehow or other now that I'm a Christian, I don't give problems to anyone any more.

I stood there watching him make out the tickets, and was thoroughly convinced he must have had a fight with his wife that morning, because somehow or other I KNEW that he was misdirecting my luggage. Normally I would have prayed and asked God to see that the luggage got on the plane, but for some reason or other, I just wasn't led to do this, so I stood there knowing full well he was misdirecting my luggage.

I took my claim checks and walked down and got on the plane and didn't even bother praying to see that the luggage got on, and didn't even look out the window to see if it was, because I knew it wasn't, so I just said, "Praise the Lord, give thanks for all things, because all things work together for good for those who love the Lord and are called according to his purpose," fastened my seat belt, and waited for the takeoff.

The flight was uneventful for a while—dinner was served on the plane, and since I was sitting in a seat by myself I assumed that the Lord didn't have anyone in particular he wanted me to talk to that day, so I read my Bible for a little while and then all of a sudden I felt a tremendous compulsion to get up.

I didn't know why, but all of a sudden I KNEW I had to get up (I really felt like I had bugs crawling all over me) so I got up and started to walk to the rear of the plane. Just as I had reached about the third seat from where I was sitting, I saw a gentleman on the plane get up, hesitate for a minute, and then he just stood by his seat.

People really aren't strangers on a plane, and I never know which one God has prepared for me, and since I never want to pass up an opportunity, I made the grand statement, "Hi!" And so he in return said "Hi!" I just mentioned to him that I had felt real "wiggly" in my seat and had just had an urge to get up and he said he had felt the same thing, but couldn't figure out what it was.

20

We laughed over this apparently nonsensical "coincidence" and I asked him if he was from Miami, and he replied that he lived in St. Louis, Missouri, but that he had been working in the Miami area and was on his way home. Then, to be polite, he asked me if I lived in Miami. And after I had answered that I did, he asked me the next follow-up question, which was, "Are you going somewhere on a business trip?"

Well, that was the opening that the Lord had prepared for me, so I began to share with him the fact that I had not become a Christian until I was forty-nine years of age, and most astonishingly I made a statement I have never made to anyone while witnessing. I said "I didn't know what the word 'saved' meant until I was that old!"

I had really begun praying for the power of God's Holy Spirit to fill me to give me the right words to say and the conversation continued in this vein: "Saved? You mean I'm lost?" And even though this has never been a word I use with non-Christians, I teasingly said, "Well, Mister, if you're not 'saved' you'd better believe you're lost." Then I added, "And if you've never been 'born again,' you'd better believe you're lost."

God's Holy Spirit had so done a job and had so prepared his heart, that he asked the most leading question in the world. He said, "How do I get 'born again?'" Well, to anyone who has any concern over lost souls, this is the most beautiful question in the world. But just about this time the seat-belt sign flashed and he grabbed my arm and said, "Don't go back to your seat—stay and tell me about being 'born again.'" So we sat down in the rear seat of the plane, and since I always "happen" to have copies of the 4 Spiritual Laws with me (tucked conveniently in my purse, my pockets, my shoes, etc.) I got one out real quick, but because of the noise of the engines by this time I decided not to read

21

the booklet, but gave one to him and asked him to read it, because it would explain how to be "born again."

When he turned the page to where the prayer is, I simply said, "Would you like to ask God to forgive your sins and ask Christ to come into your life?" And as I turned to look at him, I saw tears trickling down his cheeks, because God's Holy Spirit had done the job, and he said to me, "I prayed that little prayer while you were talking to me just then."

I thought he might be teasing me, so I said, "O.K., then, where is Christ right now?" And he said, "I'll bet you think He's in your heart, but He's in *my* heart." Then he asked me an interesting question. He said, "Do you have another copy of this little booklet I could have for my wife? She's not a Christian either, and I'd like to 'born her again' tonight." I said, "P.T.L.—you'd better believe I do." So I gave him another copy of the little booklet. Then he related to me that he was going to call an aunt in San Diego that night because she had spoken to him about religion for years, but he said it never made any sense to him until I spoke to him that afternoon.

Then he made a most unusual statement, because he said, "When you walked down the aisle of the plane as I had to stand up, I KNEW that something *religious* was going to happen to me." P.T.L. for that "old-time religion" which believes in the power of God's Holy Spirit and letting *God* do the work.

He got off in St. Louis and I continued on to Tulsa, and by this time I was really on a spiritual cloud, because there is nothing that thrills me like seeing someone else have the "light" turned on in their life. And as I sat and looked out of the window before arriving in Tulsa, I saw a beautiful lighted cross standing out plainly in the dusk of evening. I said, "Thank You, Lord, for letting me see a cross at the start of this trip, because I just *know* great things are going to happen all the way."

I later discovered that it wasn't a man-made cross at all, but God's Holy Spirit had allowed me to see a cross in the intersection of the two streets of a very small town outside of Tulsa.

The big jet set down in Tulsa, where I was met by a pastor and his wife whom I had never seen before. They had booked me into their church at the suggestion of their youth minister, so I greeted them and they welcomed me to Tulsa, and then I said, "There's no point in looking for my luggage, because I'm sure it was misdirected in Miami." But we went to check anyway, and sure enough, no luggage! We checked into the airline counter and after an hour of checking for the luggage it couldn't be found, so the airline clerk told us to go on to the pastor's house and they would call us as soon as it was located.

His "don't call us—we'll call you" sounded ominous to me concerning my luggage, so when we got out to the pastor's car, I said, "Let's pray real quick." We held hands in the car and I very simply prayed and asked God to get my luggage to Tulsa that very night. (Doesn't everybody pray for luggage?)

The pastor had told me I was to speak at a high-school assembly that next day and I knew that the right kind of clothes were important to communicate to young people. So I asked God to please see that my luggage arrived in time, and then I merely thanked Him for the way he was going to do it. I didn't know how, but I just thanked Him for whichever way He was going to do it.

I often wonder what the reaction of the pastor and his wife was toward someone who prayed for suitcases to be returned. We went on to their house anyway, had a cup of coffee, and when no call had come in, the pastor finally suggested that we call the airline, which he did, and then I talked to the clerk, who said, "Well, we finally located your luggage—it was misdirected. It's

23

locked up in Ozark Central's depot in Dallas, Texas. They don't stay open all night, but will open at eight in the morning, and we have it on the teletype to put your luggage on the nine-thirty flight in the morning, so it will be in Tulsa before eleven and will be delivered to your house by noon."

I said, "I'm sorry, but that's too late! I have to have it tonight because I'm speaking at the high school tomorrow morning and I simply must have my clothes!" He said he was sorry because there wasn't anything he could do because the airline that would bring it tomorrow was closed for the night.

I felt a little dejected and asked if I could use the washer and dryer to wash out the suit I had on, but all of a sudden I said, "Lord, I prayed in faith believing that You would get that luggage here, so I'm not going to wash out my suit, because I BELIEVE You'll answer my prayer."

Fifteen minutes later the telephone rang and the clerk said, "You'll never believe this." I said, "Oh, yes I will" (because I knew the Lord was working). And he said, "Your luggage 'accidentally' got on an American liner and is now in Tulsa and we're putting it in a cab and sending it on to you." I said, "PRAISE THE LORD!" ... and he really yelled, "What did you say?" I said "Praise the Lord"—and that's exactly what I meant, because I'd like to give you a little technical information.

The fastest time jet-wise between Dallas and Tulsa is forty-five minutes, and yet fifteen minutes after I had been advised that my luggage was visibly seen locked up in Dallas, it was in Tulsa. I felt like Peter did when he got out of jail—he couldn't understand how it happened, but he believed! And so do I believe in that "old-time" religion where God does the impossible.

The Lord knew I needed the right clothes for the assembly the next morning, and He was SOOOOO right.

It just so happened that this was the day of the high school's first football game and they were having a rally that day.

My heart really sank as I entered the high school, because all I could think of was the fact that if I were a typical high-school student, and this was the day of my high school's first football game, I sure wouldn't want to have to listen to some old lady talk about a very old-fashioned subject like religion. They were screaming madly all over the place with the pep club leading cheers and yells and the auditorium just jumping with the excitement that only the first football rally of the year can bring.

One of the things I learned early in my Christian life was a total dependence on God. I guess I learned the hard way that I can really mess things up, but if I just let God do it, it would come out just great. As I was introduced, I said the words that I always say just before I speak, "Lord, You're on"—and then I added, "You'd better be clever today, or I have a feeling they're not going to like us!" God's Holy Spirit nudged me, reminding me that it was my daughter's high school's first football game of the season as well as Tulsa's, so I asked them if they would mind giving a cheer for my high school, just to keep me from feeling lonesome since I couldn't be there. They were so worked up they would have yelled for anything, so they gave a real big cheer: "Yeah, Miami-Killian High School."

I never waste time when it comes to talking about Jesus Christ, and I never beat around the bush, so I didn't that day either, but came right back after the big cheer with, "If you'd yell that loud for the cause of Jesus Christ, you'd turn the world upside down!" Then I spoke for a while, relating some of the real exciting stories that I reserve for young people, and all of a sudden I looked at the football team sitting there on the front row.

25

Did you ever really look at the football team during a rally? They all sit there like a bunch of bumps on a log, arms folded—shoulder pads protruding all the way across from seat to seat, and just generally looking real important.

I have never understood why the football team doesn't do something at a rally except just sit there, so all of a sudden I looked at them because everyone else had been so wound up about everything, so I said, "Stand up!" . . . And you know what happened? . . . they all stood up. (It's amazing what happens when you go in the power of God.) I said, "I don't know what you yell when you make a touchdown, but tonight when you make your first touchdown, will you yell P.T.L.? Praise the Lord?" And do you know what they said? They said "Yes!" (I think they were stunned.) So I said, "O.K., sit down!" And so they sat down.

The principal of the high school ran up on the stage and said, "I move we make Frances an honorary member of the football team because she's the only woman in history who ever got a football team on their feet during a rally," and since they unanimously voted, I was made an honorary member of the Sandites Football Team of Sand Springs, Oklahoma.

Now it isn't every day that an old gal like me gets made an honorary football player, so I was really thrilled, but that was nothing in comparison with what followed. Immediately after the rally the sponsor of the pep club came up and asked me to come to the football game after the church service that night and to sit with the three hundred or four hundred girls in the pep club. I replied that I would be delighted to, so after the church service, the pastors and several members of the congregation and I went to the football game.

They led us onto the field, and as we walked down the field the stadium rocked with a cheer: "Give her a

26

'P' (clap), 'T' (clap), 'L' (clap)—Praise the Lord." I was so stunned I couldn't believe my ears, so I turned to the pastor, and it was mass confusion as both of us said, "Did you hear what I heard?" And he said, "It sounded to me like P.T.L."—and I said, "It sounded to me like 'Praise the Lord.'" I guess they saw we were so confused over what we heard that they gave the cheer again and we knew then that somehow or other God is at work with young people today because He must have communicated that morning at the assembly.

If that doesn't give you spiritual goose pimples, the sponsor of the pep club ran out to meet us and put a pair of binoculars in my hand and said, "Look at the football team—look at the football team!" I looked through the binoculars and on the helmet of every football player in Sand Springs, Oklahoma, were printed three letters. Would you like to guess what they were? You're right . . . P.T.L.*

CHAPTER IV

Praise the Lord—For Delays

GOD GIVES US opportunity after opportunity to discover that if we praise the Lord in all circumstances it will turn out to be a blessing. On a tour which was completed just before the Christmas holidays, a tremendous snow storm and fog came up during the night, and when I called the airport in the morning to make sure my plane was on schedule, I discovered they had canceled all the flights. It was pretty difficult to say Praise the Lord at that moment because I had been away from my family for ten days, and I was anxious to get home, but

---

*Author's note: I told them afterward they should have put an "A." after the P.T.L. on their helmets (Praise The Lord Anyway)—they lost the game!

nevertheless I said, "Praise the Lord," remembering what the Bible says.

The airport called me back and told me that even though the airport at Bloomington, Illinois, was closed, the one at Peoria, Illinois, was open if I could get someone to drive me the fifty miles over there. As always, the Lord came through, and a fabulous Christian lady drove me over to the Peoria airport. My plane there was right on time, and I was thrilled as we flew into the Chicago airport, where I was to make a connection to bring me home to Houston.

I checked in as quickly as I could, and sat down to await the arrival of the plane which was coming from Portland, Oregon. I opened my Bible and began reading, saying, "Thank You, Lord, for getting me to the Chicago airport and for giving me time to really refuel after all the giving out I've been doing in the last ten days." I was perfectly content just drinking in God's word, but all of a sudden I became aware of the fact it was longer than it should have been before boarding the plane, so I went up to the desk and asked the young man when we would be boarding.

He smiled very apologetically and told me that the plane was coming from Portland, Oregon, and had been grounded because of a bad snowstorm there, so it would be at least one hour late arriving and thus we would be one hour late taking off for Houston.

I sat down and continued just absorbing God through His Holy Word, thinking it wasn't too bad because we were going to be an hour late, and thanking him for giving me this special time to read my Bible. The hour passed, and I still couldn't see any plane outside the gate where we were scheduled to depart, so once again I went up to the desk and inquired about the anticipated time of departure. Again the young man said apologetically that the plane was having trouble with the storm

28

in the Portland area, and it looked like it was going to be two hours late.

Well, you guessed it, the two hours turned into three and the three into four, and I was still sitting in the Chicago airport saying "Thank You, Lord." Now it was amazing what this did to me as a person. I wasn't the least bit frustrated because of the delay and yet there were lots of reasons I could have been frustrated. I could have been irritated because I had been separated from my husband and my daughter for ten days, and now everything "seemed to go wrong" just to delay me and make it longer before I could see them. I could have been irritated because sitting in an airport for several hours on hard plastic seats isn't the most joyous thing in the world, and I could have complained about that, but somehow or other because I believed that "all things work together for good for those that love the Lord and are called according to His purpose," no irritation or annoyance crept in.

I temporarily put my Bible down because I was aware of the conversation of other passengers. I wish you could have heard them! Such swearing and frustration, it was unbelievable. Dispositions frayed, people complaining to each other, and everyone really beginning to gripe about the airlines. Instead of thinking how many times they had flown right on schedule, each one was telling the other about some one particular flight where they had been delayed, and it was amazing to see how upset many of the people became. They paced up and down, smoking one cigarette after the other, losing their tempers, and taking a lot of their resentment out on the young man at the desk (who really had nothing to do with the entire situation except to relay the right information), and in general making themselves miserable.

I used all the available time to cram on the word of God, and the more I read the more peaceful I became.

Finally the clerk announced that there was a flight for Dallas boarding and if we would hurry some of us might be able to get on it, and from there we could catch a plane to Houston. I thought, "Great, anything to get out of this snowy country to any town where I can catch a plane to Houston," so along with the scowling mob I went over to try and get on the Dallas plane. The Lord really blessed and I was one of the stand-bys who made it on the plane. So I looked around and said, "Well, Lord, is there someone on this plane You want me to talk to? Is this the reason for all the delay in Chicago?" But as I discovered my seat number, I found out the woman sitting next to me couldn't speak English, and I couldn't speak whatever was her native language, and sitting next to her was her little boy, so that wiped out sharing Christ with them.

We got to Dallas and I prayed the Lord would give me time enough to call my husband again and let him know what flight I was on, and sure enough, as we were running between the two planes, I spied a phone booth, made a call, and went right through to him, advising him that I was in Dallas and on the way home.

We boarded the plane at Dallas and as soon as it was filled, we started to take off, and one engine "froze." I said, "Well, thank You, Lord, again. I don't know why the extra delay, but I'm sure there's a good reason for it." Again, you could hear the others in the plane beginning to grumble about the additional delay. About this time the stewardess came through and announced that everyone would receive a free cocktail because of the delay.

Funny how people think this will relieve the tension of a situation when only Christ can really do a good job. As she asked the two other people sitting with me, the woman said, "I'll have a Manhattan," and nothing happened, but the man who was right next to me said, "Make mine a martini." And as he said those words, I knew why God had put me on this particular plane. The minute he had uttered the word "martini" I remembered all the martinis I had drunk in my life before I became a Christian, and said "Thank You, Lord," and opened the conversation by saying, "I used to be a martini drinker, but not any more." The young man said, "Oh, no? How come?" Fabulous opportunity for witnessing, so I began to share with him how I had found the answer to life to be in a man named Jesus Christ and not in a martini glass or anything else of the world. I just shared with him briefly how I had become a Christian at the age of forty-nine and how Jesus Christ had completely transformed my very being and then I asked him if he had ever heard of the 4 Spiritual Laws, the little tool I use to present Christ to people.

Since he had never heard of them, I began to read out of the booklet, and when I finished I asked him if he would like to become a Christian, and his answer gave me the positive assurance that God had arranged the entire thing because he said, "Three years ago I heard Bobby Richardson talk and I saw that he had a special something in his life that I didn't have, and ever since then I've been wanting the same thing, and when you started to talk to me, I realized instantly you had the same thing. Yes, I do want to become a Christian, but I just never knew how."

Isn't it amazing what God can do with a situation if we will just say P.T.L.A. (and mean it) and wait to see what God's got planned. God had prepared the heart of someone very special who was searching for someone to tell him the answer to the God-shaped vacuum in his life.

Isn't it beautiful just to know that ALL things do work together for good for those that love the Lord and are called according to His purpose? When we let our own ego get in the way, and we get back on the throne of our life and forget the promises that God has for us, we pass up the opportunities He gives us, because we are not in the proper relationship to Him to be able to see and make the most of the fabulous things He does.

CHAPTER V

P.T.L.A.
(Even When Church Is Over)

I ALWAYS HATE to see a church service come to a close. Somehow or other, we've all put aside the cares and problems of the world and have given all of our attention to the things of God, and many people don't do this all week long except for a short time on Sunday, so I always hate to see it over, because I'm concerned about those who might not even think about God again until the next Sunday morning.

I'm a great one for feeling that you ought to come out of church high on a mountain-top—I think every church service should make you feel that you want to stop everyone on the highway on the way home and tell them about Jesus Christ and what He can do for a life. I just feel so effervescent upon leaving church, it's hard for me to contain my joy, and many times people have been disappointed because someone hasn't made a public commitment of their life by going to an altar during the invitation, but I've found that these situations many times can be a P.T.L.A. (Praise the Lord Anyway).

I'm just going to share a few of these stories with you and show you what happens to turn a P.T.L.A. into a P.T.L. if we just keep our eyes open.

The church service was over, people were making their way to the back of the church to shake hands with the pastor and hurry home to dinner after an exciting service. The organist had left, the pianist was gone, and the church was almost empty, when I saw her. She was a young girl, probably eighteen or nineteen years old, who had sat through the service but had not responded to the invitation given at the end of the sermon. Yet as I looked at her, and saw the tears streaming down her face, I knew that God had spoken to her during the service.

My heart was so full of love it just spilled over—I couldn't help it, and softly I said, "Did God talk to you this morning?" The tear-stained face turned toward me and said, "Oh, yes, He really did!" Then I said "Would you like to accept Christ as your Savior and Lord right now? You can sit right down here in the pew, or we'll go to the altar and ask God to forgive you and ask Christ to come into your heart, if that's what you want." She said, "Oh yes, that's what I want—can I really pray right here in the pew?" I said, "Why, certainly, it doesn't make any difference WHERE you pray, it's just what's in your heart that counts."

We sat right back down in the pew, and with the church almost empty, we prayed as she asked God to forgive her sins, and then she became radiant as she asked Jesus Christ to come into her heart and live His life through her.

From 18 to 88

My husband and I had been in a very tiny little church where we felt the Lord had called us, and we had such an exciting time as we shared with this little backwoods church, which never had any visiting "celebrities," as they called us. Their love and warmth were almost unbelievable as we spent a Saturday evening and Sunday with them.

We started our services on Saturday night in this little church and one old man sat there listening intently to the entire service, but when the invitation to come forward was given he didn't respond in any way, but he had been so intent I felt he must be a Christian.

On the way out, as I shook hands with him, I said, "I have a feeling you've been a Christian a long time." He looked at me rather quizzically, and then to continue the conversation, I said, "How long have you been a Christian?" He looked back at me in wonderment as he said, "I don't even know if I am a Christian!" My heart nearly pounded right out of me, because I knew he had to be close to ninety years of age, and I said, "You don't *know* if you're a Christian? All I can say is you're getting up in years, and you'd better make sure that you KNOW you're a Christian before anything happens to you." I was so concerned because of his advanced age, and I didn't want him to leave that building without KNOWing that he was a Christian.

My husband immediately followed this old gentleman out of the church and explained to him that his years of churchgoing were to no avail until he actually was "born again," and so in the darkness outside the church, he prayed and asked God to forgive him of a lifetime of sins, and then he asked Christ to come into his heart.

He came to each of the remaining services while we were there, and listened intently to each one, and that might have been the end of the story except for a letter we got from one of the members of the congregation a month or so later.

It said "You remember, Charles, the 88-year-old man you talked to after the service Saturday night? We had a time of sharing just what your meetings had meant to each of us on Sunday nite. The pastor asked this man for his testimony. He said, 'I just don't understand it at all and I will never say I KNOW I will go to heaven. Maybe some day I will understand.' The Sunday before we left for Florida this man came to the altar and wept and really came through and now he can say he is SURE where he will spend eternity. PRAISE GOD!"

After the church service was over in a huge church in a metropolitan area, a little girl of six or seven years ran up to me, put a note into my hand, and then ran off to get in the car with her parents. After the church had emptied, I opened the little note, which said: "I love your sermons, I understand you. Will you go to the altar with me tonight? I will pray for you as you are going back home. I will miss you. And I love your stories too. And remember, have faith, and PRAISE THE LORD!"

As soon as I read the note, I ran to see if I could find her, feeling the time to pray was RIGHT NOW, but I couldn't find her, so I anxiously awaited the evening service, and sure enough, she was right there, sitting on the front row. My heart just jumped with joy when I saw her, and before we ever started singing the invitation song, she was right at the altar, crooked her little finger at me, and as I went down to the altar and bent over her, she said, "Did you read my note after church?" Thrilling to know that God speaks even to small children in unforgettable ways.

I had been speaking to a young people's group on witnessing and how to share your faith, and God communicated that we should give everyone there an opportunity to pray to receive Christ, because witnessing certainly can't be successful if you're not a Christian yourself, so I did, but I still felt God speaking about a certain young man. As soon as the service was over, I stepped over to where this young man was standing, and with great love which God was giving me, I simply asked him if he was a Christian.

I knew that God had been speaking to him and yet somehow or other I felt he had not prayed the sinner's prayer with the rest of the young people. He was honest and said, "No, ma'am, I'm not a Christian." He was rebellious—probably fifteen years of age—long curly hair and a real defiant look. I said, "How come—I think anyone's a real nut who's not a Christian, because what God can do in a life is fantastic!" Then I added, "I'll bet you think you have to give up doing everything you think is fun, don't you? I'll bet you think your life will be miserable from then on, don't you?" He sheepishly admitted this was true.

I talked to him a little bit longer, and then asked him if he wouldn't like to pray right there, and God had so enveloped him with His love, he began to sob, and prayed right on the spot.

The morning service which followed the youth service was most interesting, because the evangelist preached on the story of Philip and the eunuch, and how Philip had been obedient to God when He told him to go down to the desert of Gaza. Philip didn't argue and tell God that the climate and everything was much nicer where he was than it was in Gaza, but down to Gaza he went. The church service was over, and the eunuch was riding along in his chariot reading from the book of the prophet Isaiah. Then the Holy Spirit said to Philip, "Go over and walk along beside the chariot," so Philip ran over and heard what the eunuch was reading and asked him if he understood it.

Church was over—he had been to Jerusalem to worship at the temple and his answer was like the boy's that day, "Of course not!" And then he told Philip he couldn't understand it and asked him to come and sit in the chariot with him. So Philip (after the church service was over) turned a P.T.L.A. into a P.T.L. by telling the eunuch about Jesus, and the eunuch was converted on the spot.

Philip changed the negative minus to the plus or cross of Jesus Christ. It was hard to believe that we had

36

just been through an exact parallel in 1970. Compare the two stories and see how identical they are in purpose, pattern and follow-up! Isn't it fabulous to know that the same things happen today exactly as they did when the Bible was written?

At a convention recently, the service ended, and suddenly people swarmed up to the microphone to testify what Christ had done for them, or to lay a special request before the congregation. One woman who came up to the microphone had driven 1,200 miles because she was concerned about a drunken brother-in-law and an alcoholic sister.

She asked the entire congregation at the camp meeting to pray that God would give her the courage to drive over to a town some fifty miles away and get her sister and brother-in-law and bring them back to the camp meeting. I immediately took the microphone back again and asked the entire congregation to pray INSTANTLY that this woman would have the courage to go, and to pray that God would prepare the hearts of her family to receive God's word when she brought them back to the camp meeting.

A few hours later I was completing a youth service when someone indicated to me that the people we had prayed for were on the camp grounds in the car with the sister who had asked for courage. I immediately grabbed an exciting Christian young man to accompany me, and I ran down to the car. I certainly was not prepared for what greeted me!

I had walked up on the man's side of the car, and just started a casual conversation with him, waiting for God's Holy Spirit to give me the green light to start really talking in earnest about Christ, when the woman in the car began swearing in a very foul manner. I really prayed for patience and love. The woman was so drunk she could hardly sit up and the man was not much better, however she was so belligerent I think I prayed for love for her more than anything else.

Had I not been a Christian, I would have certainly left her company, feeling that no one had to put up with that kind of filthy talk, but it's an amazing thing what God's love can do—I felt great compassion for this pathetic woman, and God told us to love the unlovely. I tried to communicate with her, but in her drunken stupor I could not communicate at all, when all of a sudden God's Holy Spirit indicated that the husband was the one whose heart had been prepared.

I started talking to him, and the woman really cursed me in a tirade that made my hair stand on end, but I kept sending "love" thoughts to her while talking to her husband. Finally, the woman began to get sick and the Lord sent someone over who took her out of the car and helped her to a rest room.

God's Holy Spirit simply enveloped the entire car, and all of a sudden the man confessed that he had been thinking that he had better "get right with the Lord" because recently he had realized that he was getting older and the prospect of hell made him realize the necessity of finding God.

It was so thrilling to sit in the car and listen to him pray, asking God to forgive him of his sins, and then asking Christ to come into his heart. He then asked God to use him to win others to Christ. He then put his "booze and cigarettes" on the altar and asked God to remove them.

I always feel if a person is truly converted, the first thing they will want to do is to share the GOOD NEWS with someone else, and the first thing this man said was, "Give me another one of those 4 Spiritual Law booklets —and don't worry about my wife—I'll convert her!"

The thing that amazed me the most about the entire situation was the fact that because of God's love I could keep on loving this most unlovely woman. I have never seen such hate as she had, nor such a vicious tongue, and yet God protected me with an invisible shield.

I wonder how many times we fail to be a Good Samaritan because of our own human nature being repelled by some very unlovely person, and yet if we surrender all to God, He, and He alone, can give us the power to love.

CHAPTER VI

P.T.L.A. for Your Opportunities

—In a Factory

I HAD JUST finished speaking at a woman's luncheon and had to really move to be able to make it to a neighboring town some forty miles away where I was scheduled to speak that same night. The pastor of the church where the luncheon was held had asked one of the guests, who worked in a town beyond where I was going for the night, if she would take me to my next stop. She agreed, saying if I didn't mind driving out to her farm with her so she could change clothes, since she worked in a factory.

I went along, but when we got to the town where I was to speak for the night, she was horrified to discover that she had left the key to the trunk of her car in the coat which she had changed at home to get into her factory clothes.

As I always do in times of crisis, I said, "Praise the Lord, give thanks for all things, because all things work together for good for those who love the Lord." The poor girl looked at me like I was a real nut, because she couldn't take me back home, since she had to get to her job at the factory, so I assured her that she shouldn't worry, because the pastor would be glad to take me back, and anyway I knew that God would perform a miracle out of this.

After locating the minister I told her that after we had gone out to her home and gotten the key, we would go to the factory, pick up my luggage, then we would return the key to her. This entailed driving quite a few miles, but we made it in good time and all the while I was wondering how the Lord was going to use this for a miracle, but I was confident that somehow God would be glorified through all this confusion and extra mileage.

When we drove into the factory parking lot, we spotted the woman's car, and as we drove up close to it I could see a little note Scotch-taped onto the back of it. I excitedly squealed: "Here's the miracle, here's the miracle!" We jumped out of the car and the note said, "Bring the key in through the double door." I started up the ramp into the factory, through the double doors which were open, and then through another little door which led right into the factory. It was a factory which made timers for washing machines, and I was intrigued as I stood there for a moment watching the conveyor belts, and the lights flashing, etc. I finally spotted the woman who had driven me and I ran down to give her the key to her trunk.

To show you how God was working in this situation, at this particular moment, an emergency meeting of all the supervisory personnel of the factory had been called, and there was not one supervisor on the floor! I was excited because as I looked at the girls on the production line I wondered which one God had chosen for His kingdom that very day. I returned the keys, then backed up on the production line and asked the next employee what her particular job was, but I got no green light from God, so I went on to the next employee and got nothing. I went to the third, then the fourth, then the fifth, and still nothing, but I was still confident that God had a miracle waiting for me in that factory somewhere.

I had been carrying a copy of my book *God Is Fabulous* with the name side out, and as I started for the sixth girl, the girl across the conveyor belt said to me, "That's a pretty book you've got there. Did you write it?" Instantly the green light flashed, and I said, "Yes, but the story inside is much prettier than the cover. Would you like to read it?" She said she would, so I leaned all across the conveyor belt and gave it to her, then I stepped back and said, "It's not autographed— I'll come over there and autograph it for you." Feeling that a point of contact was necessary, I had used this as an excuse to get over to her side of the conveyor belt.

I ran all the way down to the end of the factory, and then ran back up to where she was, and while I am normally more subtle, this time I simply said, "This tells the story of how I became a Christian at the age of forty-nine. Are you a Christian?" And she replied, "No, I'm not! I'm so awful that I couldn't be a Christian." I told her that it didn't make any difference how awful she was, that God could forgive her sins faster than she could snap her fingers, and after that she could ask Christ to come into her heart.

It was a most unusual situation, because in a factory like this, all these little parts come down the conveyor belt, and the girls pick one up, put it on the tester, and, if it tests O.K., put it back on a conveyor belt and reach for the next one. If however, it should be defective, red lights flash on, a pencil must be picked up, and they write a "1" down to indicate a defective item, then remove the timer from the tester and put it over into a box on the other side. This really requires concentration to make sure you remember what you're doing, and all the time I was talking to the girl I asked her if I was bothering her and keeping her from her work, because I was very worried that I would hold up production, but she wasn't getting behind on the timers, and seemed to be doing her job, so I kept right on talking, telling her

41

what Christ could do in her life if she would be willing to surrender and let him take over.

I read the 4 Spiritual Laws to her and at the end asked her if she would like to pray the prayer, and she said "Yes," so with the red and green lights flashing, she prayed and asked God to forgive her of her sins, and then asked Christ to come into her life.

I continued talking to her for a little while, telling her of the necessity of digging into the Scriptures and also of getting herself into a good church, and all of a sudden I felt a huge hand on my back. God's Holy Spirit had so engulfed us that all I could think of was, "Who's this barging into my spiritual world" but before I could even turn around a gruff voice said, "What do you think you're doing here!" I guess I've never had time to learn to pray formally because I'm always getting myself into spots where I have to really scream for God, so while I silently screamed for God to tell me what to say I mentally had a picture of me in jail with Paul and Silas.

But instead of panicking, I turned around very quietly and said the only thing God's Holy Spirit had planted in my mind, "I'm sorry! I'm a Christian, and I wouldn't ever deliberately do anything wrong. I hope I haven't hurt Debbie's job." I explained that I was autographing a book I had written, and then I asked him if he would like to have a copy and he said he would love to. God's Holy Spirit melted the superintendent down and he said, "Oh, that's all right honey," I quickly finished autographing the book, bid Debbie a fond farewell and left.

I ran out to the car for another copy of my book to autograph for the plant superintendent and when I came back in I realized that I had forgotten his name, so I asked one of the employees standing there what the plant superintendent's name was, and as I bent down to personally autograph the book for him, another hand hit me across the back saying, "Don't you know it's against the law to be in a factory with moving parts? What are you doing here!"

I nearly dropped right in my tracks, and this time I knew beyond a shadow of doubt I would probably end up in jail, but it seemed all God told me to do was to say, "I'm autographing a book for the plant superintendent, would you please tell me how to spell his name?" All of his gruffness left as he bent over me and spelled out the superintendent's name. I thanked him profusely and told him to be sure and read the book after the superintendent had finished it, and he said he would love to.

I just say "PRAISE THE LORD" for a situation which permits the Spirit of God to move even in a factory so that people can be made aware of their needs. And just as an afterthought you might be interested in knowing these girls are now having Bible-study groups meeting weekly, and the plant superintendent has asked me to come back and share Christ with all the employees the next time I am in the area.

—In a Filling Station

Praise the Lord God never lets us down. My husband and I had been conducting a seminar on witnessing in a small eastern town, and everyone had been given cards prepared by the pastor, and we were making calls to share Christ with individuals. We had gone together because there was a divorced woman the pastor wanted us specifically to talk to, so we sent everyone off on their calls, and we started out.

He felt this would be a real productive call because the woman had indicated a real need and a real searching, so we excitedly located the house and went and knocked on the door. We had seen a sign on the fence which said "Beware of dog" and we just prayed a quickie prayer asking God to watch over us concerning the dog.

43

When we rang the doorbell we were floored to see a man come to the door, so we asked for the woman by name, and he said she was out, but that he was her husband. We talked for a few moments, and then decided to talk to him about Christ, and before we had gone very far we got a very emphatic "I'm not the least bit interested!" and then an abrupt indication that we should leave right then and there. We looked at the dog, noted that the man had been drinking heavily, and agreed with the man that we should leave right then and there.

We got in the car, and I looked at my husband and simultaneously we said, "PRAISE THE LORD ANYWAY." Then we laughed and said, "Praise the Lord the dog didn't bite us." We were disappointed, though, because we had only been given two cards because of the shortness of time and the fact that we were in a strange town, and we wanted to be able to go back and share some excitement of what can happen when you're willing to go out for Jesus Christ.

As we drove away we noticed the car which had been loaned to us was low on gasoline, so we decided to put some gas in while I looked at the map to see if I could find the location of the next house we were to call on.

Try as I might, I couldn't find the street anywhere on the map, and even though I might have been disappointed, I said, "Well, P.T.L.A.—guess You didn't want us to make any calls today, did You, Lord?" I was sitting in the front seat of the car and all of a sudden I heard someone say, "Did you know that God loves you and has a wonderful plan for your life?" I couldn't believe my ears (and yet I should have, knowing my husband), because it was my husband's voice and he was obviously reading the 4 Spiritual Laws to the filling-station attendant.

I really began praying that God would keep any customers out of the filling station until after Charles had finished, and before long I heard the young man praying right on the spot asking Christ to come into his heart.

When my husband got back in the car we really rejoiced because we had kept on praising God for everything, even though for the moment it didn't look like we had much to praise, but believing this really turned the afternoon into a real PRAISE THE LORD!

—At a Convention

I often think of how we as parents often play little jokes on our children somehow or other to let them know we have a real special love for them. I think of our teen-age daughter and the very special little jokes we have just between mother and daughter and the very special little teasings she has with her dad, and sometimes I wonder if God doesn't do the same things for us.

August of 1970 was to be a real exciting month for me, because I had been selected to be the pace-setter speaker for the Christian Booksellers Convention. Any author knows this is a tremendous privilege to be able to share in person with the people who are responsible for your books getting into the hands of the reading public.

Many an unknown author has been "made" by such an opportunity as this. I had been advised early in the year of my selection, and I was thrilled to death as a comparatively new author (three books to my credit, but less than two years of writing) so I bought the outfit I was going to wear months in advance and could hardly wait for the exciting opportunity.

I had been at two different churches the day before, and had rushed into the hotel late in the evening, and after a good night's sleep, the next morning was all of a sudden here, and the exciting moment I had waited for was not in the future, but in the NOW! I mounted the platform, quickly said those fabulous words I always do before I start, "Lord, You're on," and I began speaking.

Now I'm not going to share with you what I said, because for this book that's not important, but after the meeting had been dismissed, many of the booksellers came up on the platform to shake my hand, and all of a sudden, it seemed like the whole world began to fall apart. The platform very slowly, but oh so very surely, began to collapse!

The platform had been made out of folding tables, and my husband, who was standing with me, happened to be standing on another table, and so he didn't follow my downward trend. It all happened very slowly but it seemed like an eternity to me. All of a sudden, where I was standing looked like a slide, and I was on the bottom of the slide going down even further, and a woman came sliding down the incline right on top of me.

I don't really know exactly how everything happened —nor do I remember what hit what, but I do know, before it was all over, here I was, on the day of my GREAT opportunity, on the bottom of the pile! My wig flew off! My glasses flew off. And I was all of a sudden in a most undignified, unladylike position.

I grabbed for my wig (because if you've ever worn a wig, you know how grubby you look underneath without it), got it on somehow or other, but in the rush, a hunk of my own hair was hanging right down the middle of my face, and the wig was on sideways, because the bangs were over on the side.

Now I'm going to give you the same opportunity I had. What would you have said under the circumstances? Let me assure you right now that I wasn't hurt, although for that hectic moment I didn't have any idea whether I was hurt or not, but somehow or other, I remembered that God loved me, and that in spite of all the happenings in the last few seconds, He still loved me, so I just shouted, "Well, Praise the Lord ANY-WAY!"

All I could think of was to give thanks for all things, because I firmly and fervently believe that ALL things happen for good for those who love the Lord! The first words I heard were these: "She really LIVES it! Did you hear what she said? She said, 'PRAISE THE LORD ANYWAY!'"

Somehow in a way I'll never understand, God had given me an opportunity to prove to the world that even under the most undesirable circumstances we can still say, "PRAISE THE LORD"!

CHAPTER VII

Praise the Lord—
For Situations
That Are Different!

THIS IS THE story of Joey, and how God took a series of circumstances and transformed them along with a lot of lives.

I had been called into a high school where dope was a real problem, and rebelliousness and resentment were running high. The racial problem was also critical and when I walked into the school where I had been given forty-five minutes to speak of what the love of God could do in their lives, I felt like all the dynamite in the world was piled up in this one school. The undercurrent could be felt in a tremendous way and it looked like it would take only one tiny little spark to set the whole thing off.

The principal came running to tell me he didn't think the kids would listen and he was almost sorry he had asked me to come because he was afraid of some real uprising while I was speaking. I had prayed and asked God to handle the entire situation, so my only comment was a silent look to heaven with the question "God, did You hear what he said?"

The assembly was called, and the students rumbled in. They didn't file in, they rumbled in! Determined not to listen, they began scraping their feet on the floor to drown out anything I might say. I really screamed for God to take over completely, because I knew that I, as an individual, could really mess up the entire situation. It was the first time in my life I have ever been booed as I was introduced, but I said to God as I walked across the stage, "God, You'd better really have something to say to these kids, because they're not kidding."

God's Holy Spirit, who can overpower the devil any day, really enveloped the auditorium, and pretty soon you could hear all over the auditorium, "Shut up, I want to hear what she's got to say," and before too much time had passed, you could have heard a pin drop. I don't believe I ever prayed so hard in my life as I spoke, because I knew God had to really do a job this time.

On my way to this school I had prayed that God would reveal to me a very special scripture to use in such a situation as this, and as always, God came through, and the following scripture was the one I used:

"In a wealthy home there are dishes made of gold and silver as well as some made from wood and clay. The expensive dishes are used for guests, and the cheap ones are used in the kitchen or to put garbage in. If you stay away from sin you will be like one of these dishes made of purest gold—the very best in the house—so that Christ Himself can use you for His highest purposes" (2 Timothy 2:20, LNT).

God had in a very unique way given me a different way of expressing the difference between a Christian and a non-Christian, and so I put the opportunity to them to either be a gold plate for God or a garbage can (and to make it interesting, I added "with maggots in

48

it"). I invited them to a meeting on Saturday night where I'd be speaking to the youth of the city in a city-wide crusade, and as soon as I came in on Saturday night several people came running over and said, "Lay off that kid in the front row because he's out to get you. He's the dope pusher in the school." And all I said was, "Lord, did You hear that?"

Again I spoke to the young people telling them of the abundant and exciting life of a real Christian, and again challenging them at the end with the scripture quoted above, and asking them what they wanted to be: . . . "a gold plate for God or a garbage can filled with maggots." I let them pray the little sinner's prayer asking God to forgive them and asking Christ to come into their hearts silently, but it seems to me when we join the royal family of God we ought to let the world know about it, so I challenged them with the statement: "The apostle Paul said, 'I am not ashamed of the gospel of Jesus Christ,' and if you prayed that prayer, you won't be ashamed of the gospel either, and you won't be ashamed to tell the world, so which one of you has got the *guts* to stand up and say, "I prayed that prayer."

Could you guess who was the first one who stood up because I had challenged his manhood? Joey was! Joey, the one I had been told to lay off of because he was out to get me! My heart really jumped with joy. Many of the young people prayed to receive Christ that night, but as always, there are those who prefer to remain outside the kingdom of God because they think it means "giving up" so much.

I happen to love teen-agers in a very special way, because I think they're only searching for the answer to life, and in many ways we adults have failed them, so they're looking in the wrong places for the way to fill the God-shaped vacuum in their lives, only because we haven't shown them the right places in the right way.

I talked to many of the kids who hadn't accepted

Christ, but had a special burden for two of those who had not. One was a lovely little girl, fifteen years old, who had dabbled in sex, dope, liquor, and cigarettes. It was heartbreaking to imagine what could happen to a darling little girl like this. When she started to leave, I put my arm around her, kissed her on the cheek, and said, "Good night, you little garbage can. I love you anyway, but I hope you don't sleep a wink until you get right with God."

And then there was a young man whom I grabbed and hugged, and then kissed with this good-night remark: "Good night, Walter, I love you, and hope you'll be *miserable* until you get right with God."

I had asked the kids to come to church the next morning, but they all offered excuses, so I went home and really prayed that God would deal with them during the night and bring them to church the next morning, and when I got to church, guess what I saw! The first four rows of the church were occupied by about thirty-five of these kids, and right in the middle of all of them was Joey! I winked at him to let him know that I saw him, and he patiently sat through the invocation, the scripture reading, the prayer, etc., but when I got up to speak, he couldn't stand it another minute, and after I said about two sentences, he yelled out: "Hey, Fran [and he began pointing], I want ya to get dis one, and dis one, and dis one, and dis one, and dis one, and dis one, and dis one," as he pointed out everyone who had not accepted Christ. Special note: All the "saints" in the church fell off their pews! God had truly raised up a Saul of Tarsus! I said "O.K., Joey, just relax, I'll 'get 'em' in just a little while."

Invitation time came and Joey probably thinks that I'm the one that's responsible for the conversion of all the kids, but God used Joey in a beautiful way to show these kids a living Christ, but Walter was still standing in the pew hanging on for dear life. When the service was over I walked to the back and was shaking hands with the congregation when Walter came by. I grabbed him and said, "Get over here, you little garbage can, I want to talk to you." And like a meek little lamb, he came and stood right beside me. (It's amazing what you can say in the power and love of God.)

As soon as I had finished shaking hands with everyone, I turned to Walter and said, "Walter, don't you want to be a Christian?" And Walter said, "Do you want me to tell you what you did all night long? You chased me . . . up one alley and down another, up another and down another, and finally you caught me, and threw me into a garbage can, and I don't want to be a garbage can any more."

I really said, "Praise the Lord" and asked him if he wanted to pray right there or if he wanted to go to the altar. He said he wanted to go to the altar where his friends had prayed, and so we did, but as we were about halfway down the side aisle of the church, I heard a loud whistle (the kind you make with your fingers in your mouth), and I heard Joey say as he was triumphantly marching down the aisle: "Come on, fellows, Walter's gonna really get it!" They somehow or other formed a semi-circle around Walter and me as we prayed, and the minute Walter finished praying and I said, "Welcome into the royal family of God," Joey ran up, put out his hand and said, "*Brother,* put 'er there!" Can you imagine? "*Brother,* put 'er there!" How did Joey know except the Spirit of God had revealed it to him.

We had another service the same afternoon and Joey brought about twenty more kids. We saw kids with brands (freshly burned) on the backs of their hands pray to receive Christ, and then Joey began to talk to us as we were leaving to go on to another town that night. Excitedly he asked me if he could start a Gold Plate

51

Club in his high school because he said he wanted to clean out all the garbage cans that were there.

God had really raised up a Saul of Tarsus in the midst of a real running battle with the devil himself. Joey said to me, "When you told me last night that God had forgiven my sins, I thought that was nice, but when I woke up this morning and realized that God had forgiven *all* my sins, I realized for the first time in my life I was FREE, do you hear me? I'm FREE, FREE, FREE." And I repeated that beautiful verse in the Bible, "You shall know the truth, and the truth shall set you free!"

More People

I am convinced over and over that God works in many mysterious ways, His wonders to perform, and God uses all different types of situations and people to bring about His miracles; and often times He holds us right down to the wire to make His answer even more miraculous.

Charles and I had been to an all-day retreat high in a beautiful mountain setting. We had shared for about ten hours the miracles that Christ was doing in our life, and trying to share with others how to really grow in Christ, how to learn to give "all" to God to discover the abundant life that Christ offers to those who will believe.

One of our greatest joys is being able to share daily miracles that God is doing RIGHT NOW and to encourage others to find the same beautiful, but narrow road. We had been unusually blessed as the presence of God enveloped the entire room. There were probably 125 people present and the quarters were very cramped. Everyone was sitting on the floor in their casual clothes, and it was a real intimate situation where the reality of Christ could be not only discussed but His very presence felt by all concerned. It was one of the most beautiful days of my life. It was about fifteen feet

52

from the room where we were sharing to the dining room, so there was no time for privacy or talking to anyone alone, so everyone shared their burdens and joy before everyone else and it was a great time of growing for all concerned.

The windup of the retreat was a banquet which was to be over at 7 P.M. I had talked so much during the ten-hour retreat I was extremely silent during the meal and was just listening to those around me. About ten minutes till seven I realized that in just ten minutes someone would be picking us up to take us to our next speaking engagement, which was two hundred miles away, so I decided quickly that I'd better excuse myself from the banquet and go to the little girl's room.

Now watch what happened! For some reason or other (you don't think it could have been God, do you?) I turned to a lady I had not said a word to, and asked her, "Will you please take me to the rest room?" She gave me a most startled look, but immediately got up. Now the thing that is unusual is the fact that I'm really a grown woman and perfectly capable of finding a rest room by myself, but somehow or other, God had led me to ask the woman sitting next to me to take me. We got up and left the banquet hall, and started down a long corridor which led to the dorms when she said, "I'm new here myself, and I don't know my way around, but I'll be glad to help you."

As we got part way down the hall, we discovered the rest room, which was occupied, and about ten ladies were standing outside. Now the normal thing to do would be to stand in line and be number eleven, wouldn't it? But for some reason or other (again you don't think it could have been God, do you?) I got a real brilliant idea and said, "Usually plumbing runs in a straight line and I wonder if there could be another rest room on the second floor?" Looking back, I can see it had to be God because I'm not smart enough to know

53

anything at all about plumbing. She said, "I don't know, but I'll go with you to find out." I assured her this wouldn't be necessary, but she insisted on going along. When we got up on the second floor, we discovered sure enough there was another rest room, and this one was empty. As a matter of fact, there was no one on the entire second floor.

I went into the rest room, and when I came out, I was amazed to see the young lady still standing there. As I took one step toward her, her eyes grew bigger and bigger and BIGGER, and she began to step backwards. I took another step, and she took another step backwards, and by this time her eyes were like saucers.

I stood still, because I realized that something unusual was really occurring. She backed up as far as she could, until she ran into the wall at the end of the second floor, and as she did, she cried out, "I believe God is real!" Goose pimples ran up and down my spine! I ran toward her and said, "Of course, honey, God is real, what makes you so emphatic about that right at this particular moment."

The following story is what she told me:

Her husband had been killed and her world caved in and she decided there was no hope where she was concerned, so she put her children to bed and told them good-bye and drove up on the top of a mountain, to die. The woods were shut down because of the forest fire, so there wouldn't be any workers up there. She was crying, cursing, saying, "O.K., God, where are You? If You care so much, where are You?"

She said she had believed there was a God ever since she first heard of Him, but had seen more of the devil's works since then and always felt she had to fight her own battles in the way she was raised. Through stubbornness—not giving in, not quitting. But she was quitting when she went up on the mountain. She said, "If God had a plan for me He was going to have to get me off the mountain and make me know what the plan was."

After sitting in her car, which had run out of gas, in the sub-zero weather for seventeen hours, normally she would have been dead, but somehow God in His love shielded her from the cold and even though she was in an area where no one could have been expected to be, the next morning a car drove up the deserted road, saw her car covered with snow, got out, discovered the partly frozen body of a woman, and took her down to the hospital in the valley, where she recovered from the effects of the cold. God wouldn't even let her die!

Somehow or other in a way she doesn't really know, God sent someone to invite her to a retreat (the one where I was to speak) and even though she didn't want to go, she went. As Charles and I came in with our excitement about Jesus Christ, I'm sure we must have turned her off completely, talking about God's love and what He wanted to do in the life of every person there, and as she studied us, she threw out a fleece. She had sized up the situation and realized it was an impossibility to be able to talk to either of us alone, so she really put God to the test by saying, "O.K. God, if You're real, let me have a chance to talk to that woman ALONE before the retreat is over." And God had taken her all the way down to the wire, because in five more minutes we would have been gone forever out of her life, but there she was, and there I was, and we were alone on the second floor of a retreat house.

About this time I heard the noise of the banquet breaking up, and I remembered her fleece to God about talking to me ALONE, so I hurriedly glanced around, saw a broom closet at one side of the hall, grabbed her by the arm and said, "Get into the broom closet so we can pray!" (After all, the Bible does say go into the closet and pray, doesn't it?)

There, amidst brooms and mops and buckets and

55

pails, the tears of joy flooded her soul because she realized that God had answered her prayer, and she prayed and asked God to forgive her of her unbelief and she asked Jesus Christ to come into her heart. My tears really joined hers as both of us realized the awesome ability of God to whom "all things are possible."

She wrote me a beautiful letter after this happened, and I want to quote just a little part of it to you:

"When I threw out my fleece and went up on the mountain I didn't want to die—I just didn't want to live the way I have for the past three years—in limbo. I felt like a big toad—doing nothing but sitting on a rock, and I was real ripe for the devil's temptations.

"A year ago I took him up on them. To quote you, 'I was sinning and loving every minute of it.' I didn't have anything else to do. I felt like I was losing my soul, because no matter what excuses I made up, I knew God did not approve of what I was doing, so I went up on the mountain, way up, as far as I could go with the little gas there was in the car. Well, God got me off the mountain. When I met you ten days later I felt like I got a little piece of my soul back.

"The next day I went over my list of sins and since I had decided my worst sin was cussing, I was standing in the shower that morning, and I did like you said, took all my nasty words, raised them up to God, opened my hand, turned it over and watched them all run down the drain (so I thought). For twenty-four whole hours not even one little cuss word slipped out.

"*I* really felt big. Thought I had the answer to all my problems—raise them up, turn them over, and watch them run down the drain. Until the next day a little word slipped out. Just a little one, didn't think God would notice. Then it got to be a couple a day. I really got disgusted with myself and figured even God couldn't help me with that dirty habit of the tongue. (I've been cussing since I was about six.)

56

"It took me about two weeks to realize what God had really done. I was still cussing, but I hadn't spanked my kids in two weeks. Unbelievable, when you have five kids in the house. You know why I hadn't spanked them? My terrible, quick, temper was gone. That really knocked me down a peg. *I* gave God what *I* thought was my worst sin, but HE took the one *He* wanted first."

Then she closed with a marvelous statement. She said, "I know God will take care of the other problems —*I* can't solve them."

More . . . .

Many times when God begins His work of drawing us to Him, we are confronted with situations which, when we look back on them, are real "Praise the Lord Anyway" situations. My mail runs over with letters which thrill my soul, but every once in a while I get one that is so very special I want to share it with a lot of people. Such is this letter, which is shared with the permission of the person who sent it to me. Listen to how she refused to hear when God called her, how she fought it, then how she finally gave in, and look what happened. Maybe this is one that should be under the title P.T.P.A. (Praise the People Anyway) because look at how persistent God had to be in calling her to be His very own.

Dear Frances,

PRAISE THE LORD! I could write that a million times and it wouldn't be enough. God is Fabulous and I want to thank Him for using you to bring me home. You help so many that maybe you won't remember me but I pray to God that you will. I belong to the church where you spoke last Wednesday. I was introduced to you as president of your area fan club.

"Friday evening I attended your meeting in the next town, Sunday morning after you spoke I walked right into the arms of Jesus Christ. I want to tell you everything that led up to this miraculous moment in my life. I pray it will not take too much of your time to read. Your time is valuable for the Lord.

"I was raised in a church (denomination not important) which to my knowledge did not tell us the plan of salvation. I attended faithfully, so I believe that I would have heard it sometime.

"After marriage I joined my present church, which was my husband's church. That was about 15 years ago. I heard about salvation then but didn't like the idea.

"After really getting involved with church activities (of all people I was put on our Christian Education Board, which appoints teachers and decides on materials), I began to feel very needy. Something was missing! I began to search, making the common mistake of looking at others. I thought if they were really Christians (which they professed), I didn't want it. I knew I should be looking up but it just didn't work that way.

"When our new pastor came I started in a Bible-study group with his wife. Things she would say hit home. Then the owner of the book store here mentioned the novel *Christy* by Catherine Marshall. I read this and thought it was good. In the meantime our Christian Ed Comm. tried to get me to be church librarian JUST because I liked to read. They didn't realize I wasn't a Christian. I realize today that God was desperately trying to find SOMEONE who I believed was the type of Christian I wanted to be. I was given two more of Catherine Marshall's books to read by a Christian friend. They gave me quite a boost.

One day I was at our book store . . . (I can't remember why) but a clerk there recommended a book. *God Is Fabulous* by Frances Gardner (recognize this)? I brought it home and read it straight through. This Frances Gardner had something! Then I read *Go, Man, Go!* After reading the second book I was really thrilled. Here was a person who really had Jesus Christ as her personal savior. I was searching for someone who had had a Christian experience and thought it was worth letting the world know about. Not as you say, a "Secret Service Christian." *Hot Line to Heaven* came along and with it Satan telling me that maybe this woman could just write well. Satan failed. I really believed you were sincere.

Then the bookstore owners came home from the book sellers convention and told me, "Frances Gardner is just like her books." I heard the tape of your speech and I just couldn't wait for this Jesus. Well, I did wait, revival meetings came to our church, I attended three or so. One night I did get my hand up for needing prayer.

I asked Christ to come into my life and expected something great. Nothing happened. I then got a copy of the 4 Spiritual Laws which said you didn't always have a feeling till later and not everyone's experience was the same. I believe I finally accepted this. Then all of a sudden you were coming to our town and wanted to speak instead of just autographing books. I believe this was an answer to prayer.

I heard you and Charles and then was able to talk to you a few minutes afterwards. I really believed this relationship of yours with God.

Friday evening, wanting to come to the town where you were speaking, I said, "God, if You want me to go, have someone ask me to go. I was planning to drive. I expected the telephone to ring. Instead, my twelve-year-old son came to me and said he would like to hear you that night. Coincidence? I called a friend to go along who had missed you Thursday. Again you were the same.

Saturday evening I said, "God, if You want me to go to the Sunday-morning service, have my husband mention it when he comes home." He did . . . another coincidence? He said I had mentioned it in the morning but it was still an answered prayer.

We arrived just before your Sunday-school service was over. We sat in the back so we wouldn't disturb anyone. In between services we moved closer to the front. We never sit close to the front in our church. We were the front row then even though there were several empty pews in front of us. Then the pastor said you didn't like to talk to empty seats, so we moved up. I feel now that God was just getting me closer to the altar.

You spoke of your salvation, which I had read some about. I loved this talk as I had all the rest, but I felt no greater stirring than usual.

Then you had to have an altar call (P.T.L.). We misunderstood the page number and didn't find the first song, but I couldn't sing anyway. I have had my heart act up before in altar calls, but nothing like this. I made it through the four verses of that song. What a relief, but then we had to sing another one, part of the chorus "Savior while on others thou art calling, do not pass me by." The old heart was pounding.

"You said "God, let them know if they take the first step, You will take all the rest of them." More heart stuff! I prayed (by this time we were through with the third verse of this song) "God if we sing the fourth verse I'll go up." We sang it and I didn't go! We sat down while you were counseling. My heart slowed down. I prayed, "Oh, God if I could be sure I was going to the altar because of YOU and not because I admire this woman so much I would go." As you say, "WOW." I thought my heart was beating hard before. I knew I was going to have a heart attack right there if I didn't get moving. I got up (I didn't realize until later I was the last one to go that morning). I remember standing up and next kneeling at the altar. All I could think of was "Oh God, I finally made it" over and over.

Then you came to talk to me, Praise the Lord and pass the tissue. I don't believe God wanted me to cry long then, He wanted me to hear what you said. (The tears came on the way home.) P.T.L you said "What do you want?" and I answered, "Christ in my life." You led me in prayer then gave me some advice.

"Then you made a movement which made me look full in your face (I had been looking at you before this). I can't really describe this, but the love of God was shining forth from your face and you said, "Aren't you glad you've come?" I felt like God was speaking. I suppose you said something after that. I don't know.

We had been invited to my sister-in-law's for dinner along with another brother and family. We had been invited as second choice because someone else couldn't come. My sister-in-law is a Christian. Do you suppose it was a coincidence that her first choice couldn't come? I told her as soon as we got there.

On the way home I had thought I would like to say the blessing at noon but didn't say anything to her. Just before we were ready to eat she asked me in private if I wanted to say the blessing. I did. I thanked God for coming into my life and then really flubbed the rest.

Seven of us came back to hear you in the afternoon. My husband and I got to renew our wedding vows.

When talking to you afterwards I asked you to pray for our Sunday-School class party at our home the next evening. We were doing something entirely different. I had already planned to play the tape of your bookseller's speech and now I knew I would be giving my testimony.

"The next morning I went to the bookstore to pick up the tape. On the way I said, 'God, if You give me the opportunity I will tell them what happened to me.' I got the opportunity as soon as I walked in. I DIDN'T TELL THEM. I left and was crossing the street when a voice suspiciously like yours said COWARD! Needless to say I went back into the bookstore and told them.

That night as time got closer for the party I got more nervous. By the time we were to start the business meeting I had to sit down. I couldn't even go to the door, my husband had to do this alone. I had to wait until the meeting was over and I kept getting sicker and sicker. I said to myself, "why did I ever tell anyone I was going to do this?" I kept praying, but nothing helped. When I stood up I didn't have any idea how far back to start, but God knew. I started talking and I don't remember ever being so relaxed in front of people. I told everything that I have written here about that Sunday morning, and never missed or forgot a thing. It is impossible for ME to do this.

Needless to say, the Holy Spirit was present. We had that day invited an acquaintance, who had been healed of a terminal brain tumor a year before. He gave his testimony. We had not heard this before and it really meant a lot to my husband. Great things have happened since then and we expect even more.

My husband (an unsaved Christian) at that time felt rather left out of my life even though I told him he meant so much more to me now. Well, Tuesday at noon he came rushing home from work and said he wanted Jesus too. I had hoped for this, but I didn't have enough faith to believe it would be so soon. Our pastor's wife came to pray with him.

Neither one of us can believe the change in the other. It's great. We tell everyone. He tells people he's younger than me for the first time (two days).

I have been a little disappointed that others don't want to talk about Christ as much as we do. Some Christians tell us we will come down off our mountain. I believe I have leveled off somewhat and we're studying to get closer to God. We like that high and we want to stay on the mountain. Are there times when you aren't quite so high?

We would love to hear from you with any encouragement and help you might have for us. We need your prayers and you have ours. Thank you for listening to God's call to come here."

This is the story of Sam.

Sam was a cantankerous old man. Sam was sick. Sam was eighty-two years old, and the doctors didn't feel that Sam had too much time left. His little granddaughter had been converted two years before, and every day she would run up to her grandfather's bedroom and gently ask him, "Grandpa, do you want to ask Christ into your life today?" And every day for two years Grandpa would say, "I'm not ready, don't bother me now!"

I happened to be in the town where Sam lived, speaking at a Christian woman's club. I had been on an especially rugged tour, it was during the time of the year when the roads were icy and covered with snow, and driving was dangerous. I was running behind schedule and was anxious to get on my way, and yet every time we tried to get out the door, the telephone rang again. We finally decided we were going to let it ring the next time so we could get started, because as it was, I was running late for my next service, and the roads were so bad we knew it would take a lot longer than usual to deliver me to my destination.

The phone rang again. The shrill sound of the bell was like an irritating obstacle placed in front of a track runner. We started to ignore it and get in the car, but then decided it might be something important. And it was! It was Sam's daughter who asked if we might find time to stop by her home and talk to Sam before we left town to go to the next service. I looked at my watch. The time was much too late to stop, but somehow or other God said "Go!" and so we went.

We talked to the daughter for a few minutes, and then went upstairs to talk to Sam. Sam had heard the plan of salvation so many times in his life, I knew it was not necessary to go into this, so I just said, "Hi, Sam, how are you?" Sam remarked that he was miserable. Somehow God reassured me that since I was late, I didn't need to build up to anything, so I point-blank asked Sam, "Sam, are you going to heaven when you die?" Sam turned over in bed so that he didn't have to look at me any more. Then he said "No." Lovingly I said, "Sam, do you want to go to hell?" I pulled the bed away from the wall and walked around on the other side and knelt down so I could look right at Sam. He said, "No, I don't want to go to hell!" Then I said, "Well, Sam, would you like to pray and ask God to forgive you for a life of putting Him off, and ask Christ to come into your heart?" Sam came back with his usual answer, "I'm not ready." Somehow or other, the Holy Spirit had me say, "Sam, *God's ready,* even if you think you're not; don't you want to pray?" Sam looked at me and said, "Yep!" In a voice as clear and sharp as anything you ever heard Sam prayed the sinner's prayer and we all welcomed him into the royal family of God.

I got a letter just a few weeks later which I'll quote to you (with permission). "You would want to know about Sam too. He showed a gentleness and a calm (although he did not say much), after he prayed to accept Christ, that was noticeable. He grew worse and worse physically, and I went to see him on Monday, December 28, before we left town for three days, feeling that would be the last time I'd see him alive. Sure enough he went peacefully to be with the Lord on New Year's Day. We returned from our trip Sunday and heard he was gone and arrived in time for his visitation at the funeral home. We praise the Lord for what He did for Sam through you."

CHAPTER VIII

P.T.P.A.
(Praise the People Anyway)

I AM SO charged up this morning as I sit down to write, I feel just like I'll explode. Did you ever feel the power of God so strong in your life that you knew beyond a shadow of doubt that NOTHING was impossible to God? That's the way I feel this morning. But I didn't feel that way when I woke up.

I felt sluggish and drowsy—it's a fall day in Houston, rainy and dreary, and I felt just like the weather, and the thoughts went through my mind like this—"Oh, it will probably be a gloomy day all day long today—it will probably rain and I have to go to the store and I really hate to get wet."

Then I thought, "That new chair is coming for my desk today, and he probably won't get here until this afternoon, so I'll have to wait to do my shopping until late and I sure don't like that." And I probably thought a lot of other negative thoughts, and then I began to wonder how in the world God ever puts up with us. I'm sure as God looked down on me this morning He must have thrown His hands up in despair and said, "Praise the People Anyway!"

Then I started thinking in another direction because somehow God communicated to me when He threw up His hands in despair and said P.T.P.A. More and more I am convinced the devil uses fear more than anything else in the world to drag people down. It is not sickness that drags us down—it is the fear of sickness. It is not poverty that drags us down—it is the fear of poverty. It isn't tomorrow that drags us down—it is the fear of tomorrow. It isn't circumstances that drag us down—it is the fear of what the circumstances are going to do in our life that drags us down. Failure isn't what bogs us down—it's fear of failure. Old age isn't what bogs us down—it's fear of old age.

I could go on endlessly thinking of the things that we LET bog us down, but in the final analysis it's always the same—it's our lack of trust in God that allows fear to creep in our life. I believe the devil hovers over all of us constantly with a hypodermic needle full of fear, trying to inject us with a faith-destroying killer. The minute you have fear—your faith has gone down the drain and the devil knows this.

I have become a real fanatical reader of the *Living New Testament,* and today I've been so inspired by the 6th chapter of Matthew, starting with the 24th verse. "You cannot serve two masters: God and money. For you will hate one and love the other, or else the other way around. So my counsel is: Don't worry about THINGS—food, drink, money, and clothes. For you already have life and a body—and they are far more important than what to eat and wear.

"Look at the birds! They don't worry about what to eat—they don't need to sow or reap or store up food—for your heavenly Father feeds them. And you are far more valuable to Him than they are. Will all your worries add a single moment to your life? And why worry about your clothes? Look at the field lilies! They don't worry about theirs. Yet King Solomon in all his glory was not clothed as beautifully as they. And if God cares so wonderfully for flowers that are here today and gone tomorrow, won't He more surely care for you, O men of little faith? So don't worry at all about having enough food and clothing. Why be like the heathen? For they take pride in all these things and are deeply concerned about them. But your heavenly Father already knows perfectly well that you need them. *And He will gladly give them to you if you give Him first place in your life.* So don't be anxious about tomorrow. God will take care of your tomorrow too. Live one day at a time."

Think of the magnitude of that portion of scripture. So many times people take verses and meanings out of context and don't follow through to find the rich whole meaning of scripture. And all the way through the Bible, I find every single one of God's promises followed by a condition, and in this portion it is "if you will give Him first place in your life." And giving Him first place in your life means trusting Him, not worrying or stewing about "things," but trusting Him for every little detail of your life. Probably the hardest thing that people have to learn is how to trust God. People have often asked me how do you learn. Read, read, read the Bible. There is nothing that tells me more of what God wants to do for me than just getting into His word.

Many times a passage I have read over and over becomes alive NOW because that's where God is speaking to me right NOW. God meets us on our own level of understanding and reveals to us what is perfect and good for us at that moment. Maybe yesterday this scripture I have just quoted would not have been the answer to your problem, and yet today as you read it, it IS. This particular passage of scripture, however, is always the answer to any day's needs if we believe it.

Why do we worry when the Bible plainly asks if all your worries will add a single moment to your life? And when we read about not worrying about clothes, God didn't tell us that we would have to go around with clothes, because he said that King Solomon in all his glory was not clothed as beautifully as the lilies of the field.

In other words, King Solomon worried about his own clothes and provided them, but even his best did not compare with what God will give us, and He WILL give them to us because it says our Heavenly Father already knows perfectly well that you need them, and then of course He puts the condition in that we must give Him FIRST place in our life. What a glorious moment of victory when we KNOW God has first place.

Think of the excitement in your own life when you really start believing and trusting God all the way! The trouble so much of the time is that we don't really put our trust against the injections of fear that the devil gives us. If you're in business, and all of a sudden business drops a little bit, FEAR creeps in. (I shouldn't say creeps in, because the devil is never that tactful—it just barges in!)

If we don't get a prayer answered the way we want it to, fear creeps in and we don't believe that God is going to answer that prayer, but if we'd take immunization shots against fear, and trust is the immunization shot against fear, we might discover that He had already answered the prayer, maybe in a different way than we thought it ought to be answered, but in a way that was best for us, because God knows our needs even before we do.

Did you ever feel close to God when you were worrying and stewing? I doubt it. How can we be close to God when we are definitely disobeying what He tells us to do? The minute we become bogged down with worry (which is another word for fear) our contact with God lessens and His power becomes further and further away from us. Only when we put worry behind us and God in front of us does life become the fabulous experience God intended for it to be.

Whenever I read the Old Testament and read about the Israelites who saw miracle after miracle, worshiped God for a while, and then went back into their sinful ways, I wonder how many times God had to say "Praise the People, Anyway!" Aren't we exactly like the Israelites were? Put it down on a personal basis right now. We go to church on Sunday, hear an inspired sermon, come home, and then begin worrying about what we're going to have for dinner. Then we worry about how we're going to get through next week instead of relaxing and trusting God.

God performs daily miracles all around us if we will just open our eyes to see, but many times we need someone there reminding us of the daily miracles or we forget all about them. The very fact that we wake up in the morning is a miracle of God. Do we thank God for this? We ought to!

The ridiculously humorous idea just struck me as I wrote the above, how many of us could keep our bodies breathing through the night while we're asleep if it were not for God's tender mercy and care. What would happen if you had to worry about staying awake all night so you could make sure that you breathed in enough oxygen to keep you alive? How long do you think you'd last if you had to depend on yourself for your own breathing? And how much concentrating do you think you could do about your job, your school, your housework, your home, if you had to check constantly on the state of your breathing.

Isn't it wonderful that God made us with a built-in breathing system so we wouldn't have to worry? And if you don't think God did it, who do you think did it? Don't we really all have a little faith in some of God's daily miracles? Then let's start exercising MORE faith. Why not start right now reading more of God's word to see what he's got for us.

The story of Simon as told in the 5th chapter of Luke (LNT) is another story that is so relevant to to-day's living. Simon had been fishing all night and they had all worked so hard and didn't catch a thing. Then Jesus came along and said, "Go out where it is deeper and let down your nets and you will catch a lot of fish!" What would you have done if you had been Simon? Would you have said something like this: "Are you kidding? I've been out there all night long and I'm so tired I can hardly move. The fish just aren't around tonight. I'm going home and sleep and see what I can figure out myself to catch some fish." Or, "This lake is all fished out, so maybe I'll have to make my living some other way."

That's what so many of us do. We don't trust the little nudgings that God's Holy Spirit gives us, we let the devil get in there with his negative ideas, and find ourselves defeated, because trust in the devil is always defeat! But think what Simon said—and he said it so simply, because he exercised his faith: "If you say so, we'll try again." He believed Jesus. He kept his eyes on Christ and not on the problem. He kept them on the one who can solve the problem—and kept them off the problem.

Yesterday I saw a woman in a wheelchair and I felt a tremendous urge to pray for her because I believe God's

70

Holy Spirit spoke to me about this. However, because I had never seen her before and she was black, I hesitated —and this is when the devil really came in—and I thought, people will think I'm nuts if I go up to an utter stranger and ask her to let me pray for her, and so I didn't, but all night I couldn't get her out of my mind because I felt that God wanted some available person to perform a miracle through her—whether it was her body, mind or soul, I do not know, and I became unavailable because the devil put fear in my heart, but I believe God gives us opportunities all the time for miracles, and we turn away.

I asked God to forgive me and have prayed that I will never again be guilty of turning away from a miracle. How many miracles have you turned away from? Does God continually have to say about you "Praise the People Anyway" because you ignore the opportunities He gives you to be in the miracle business too?

I received in the mail a letter from a young girl who had heard me speak and she went back to her pastor and told him some of the things I had said—and some of the miracles I had related, and he said, "No one can be that close to God!" She wrote to me asking if I really was as close to God as I sounded. I assured her that all of us could be as close to God as we wanted to. I also felt that as long as her pastor had the idea he has, and doubt is in his mind about closeness to God, he will never be that close to God.

CHAPTER IX

Praise the Lord—
Right Where You Are!

I JUST BUBBLE over with real joy of knowing Jesus Christ personally, and I'm sitting here humming to my-

71

self "There's JOY in the Lord, there is joy in the Lord!" but why is it so hard for some of us to find? Over and over people tell me they wish God would use them like He uses me, and I began to wonder why God doesn't use all of us to the same degree, and a little idea began formulating in my mind.

When I first found Christ, and realized what He had saved me from, I was so excited all I could think about was sharing this with my family, which is exactly what God called me to do, and I was delighted with this fabulous opportunity He had given me, so, to the best of my knowledge and understanding at that time, I shared this with those I loved most. Some of them are Christians today, some are not, but *I was happy, because I was doing what God called me to do.*

Then one day God opened my eyes a little bit wider, and reminded me that the printing company which I owned at that time was in a shopping center, and it took me by surprise that God was going to give me such a big area to cover, but I gulped and said, "All of this, just for me?" And I set about sharing Christ with the people in the center where I worked. This was really a big job for me at the time, and *I was happy, because I was doing what God called me to do,* and in the small little world of a single shopping center I was obeying God.

Then came another day when God opened my eyes even wider, and I saw the entire town of Kendall, Florida, which is where I lived when I became a Christian, and I said, "Thank You, Lord, you've really given me a BIG job this time, haven't You?" I even told my pastor that I could share Christ every day of my life as long as I lived, and never be able to reach all the people in the Kendall area, but I immediately began doing what God called me to do, and I was happy because I wasn't trying to tell God what I wanted to do, but I was busy being obedient to the task He had laid out for me. And I would have been perfectly content sharing Christ in

Kendall the rest of my life *because it was doing what God called me to do.*

Then one day I heard God say: "How would you like the city of Miami?"—as He opened the doors of churches of all denominations to invite me to speak. I almost panicked, and said, "But, God, how about all those people back in Kendall, I haven't had time to reach all of them," but God said to go on because there were others who would fulfill the great commission in Kendall, so here *I was happy again because* even though it was different than I had originally thought it was going to be, *I was serving God in the way He wanted me to.*

Then came a little nudge one day which said, "How about the whole state of Florida?" And I said, "Who, me?" Then I went on to say, "I can't do that because I've got a business, etc.," but nevertheless I heard the small still voice of God whisper "You," so I said, "O.K., God, if that's what You want for my life, I'll do it" and so I was once again happy as new doors opened up in front of me

I had a wonderful time sharing in Florida over the weekends, and saw many exciting things happen, and probably the most exciting to me was the miracle I saw happen as God began to use me in bigger ways than I had ever dreamed of, so *I continued happy because I was doing what God wanted me to do.*

Then came a day I couldn't believe! God whispered, "You can have the whole United States" and this time I really couldn't believe it was God speaking to me, so I threw out a fleece which God answered, and all of a sudden, there I was speaking in churches, youth conventions, state camp meetings, etc., all over the United States, and I was happy, because I was being obedient to God. All I could think of was the work God had cut out for me to do by giving me all of the United States, and I knew I'd never be able to finish it in my lifetime,

73

*but I was happy because to the best of my knowledge
and ability I was doing what God called me to do.*

Then in His wonderful way, God really answered a
lifelong dream of mine. I had always wanted to visit
Hawaii, and came that day when God called me to Hawaii. I might have really questioned God this time, because the invitation to visit Hawaii was accompanied by
a letter which said, "After reading your book *Hot Line
to Heaven*, where you tell people to pray BIG, we
prayed BIG and are asking God to send you to Hawaii.
However, we can only offer you $25.00, which is our
standard speaking fee, but would you please pray and
see what God says to you?"

We prayed, and God said Go! However, God said
not only that I should go, but that I should take my entire family on a guarantee of $25.00, but he also whis-
pered "trust Me," and so in faith believing, we charged
almost $1,100 worth of airline tickets and asked God
for just two things, one thousand souls while we were
there, and enough honorariums to pay our plane fares.
And God honored both requests in a most unusual way.

Then came a call to Panama, and I might have said,
"God, You don't really mean the whole world," but I
didn't question God, but *continued to do what God
called me to do in the best way I know how, and because of this I was happy.*

Now why have I always been happy? Because I have
been satisfied doing what God called me to do. Look
back very carefully at the beginning of this chapter, and
see what I did first! I went to the first ones I thought
of—my family! And please remember that each time
God opened a wider horizon to me, I had done the job
He had previously given me to do, AND I WAS
HAPPY DOING IT. So many times we want God to
"promote" us in our own thinking to bigger and better
jobs, or at least jobs in our own mind which are bigger
and better, but what happens so many times is that God

can't give us any bigger job until we have done the first thing He's called us to do.

There would be far greater joy in the entire Christian world if we would first do what God calls us to do, without being concerned about something "bigger" and "better," if we would just realize that we've got to be obedient to the first little job God gives us to do. I often think if God had called me to spend my entire Christian life scrubbing the floor of a church, I'd have been happy doing it, because I would have been doing what He wanted me to do, so why don't you ask yourself a question right now: "Am I happy because I'm doing what God wants me to?" If not, why don't you and God have a little chat and you ask Him right now what your present job is.

Don't be surprised if the first little task God gives you is to talk to someone about their soul, because that's the only real job He has ever given us, and regardless of what God calls you to do, the ultimate purpose behind it is to point people to Christ, regardless of whether you are a Sunday-School superintendent, Sunday-School teacher, choir director, or just a member of a church, remember all jobs that you assume should point to the one main thing—the soul of man.

Don't tell God you can't talk to someone about their soul, but do it to the best of your knowledge and understanding at the present time and you'll be happy because you'll be occupying the little niche that God has prepared just for you.

Think of the story of the talents as told in Matthew in the 25th chapter (LNT). "Again, the Kingdom of Heaven can be illustrated by the story of a man going into another country, who called together his servants and loaned them money to invest for him while he was gone. He gave $5,000 to one, $2,000 to another, and $1,000 to the last—dividing it in proportion to their abilities—and then left on his trip.

"The man who received the $5,000 began immediately to buy and sell with it and soon earned another $5,000. The man with $2,000 went right to work, too, and earned another $2,000. But the man who received the $1,000 dug a hole in the ground and hid the money for safekeeping.

"After a long time their master returned from his trip and called them to him to account for his money. The man to whom he had entrusted the $5,000 brought him $10,000. His master praised him for good work. 'You have been faithful in handling this small amount,' he told him, 'so now I will give you many more responsibilities. BEGIN THE JOYOUS TASKS I HAVE ASSIGNED TO YOU.'

"Next came the man who had received the $2,000, with the report, "Sir, you gave me $2,000 to use, and I have doubled it.' 'Good work,' his master said. 'You are a good and faithful servant. You have been faithful over this small amount, so now I will give you much more.'

"Then the man with the $1,000 came and said, 'Sir, I knew you were a hard man, and I was afraid you would rob me of what I earned, so I hid your money in the earth and here it is!'

"But his master replied, 'Wicked man! Lazy slave! Since you knew I would demand your profit, you should at least have put my money into the bank so I could have some interest. Take the money from this man and give it to the man with the $10,000. For the man who uses well what he is given shall be given more, and he shall have abundance. But from the man who is unfaithful, even what *little* responsibility he has shall be taken from him. And throw the useless servant out into outer darkness: there shall be weeping and gnashing of teeth.' "

Look what the Bible says to the first man about having been faithful in handling the small amount. He was

76

given many more responsibilities. And then the order to "begin the joyous tasks I have assigned to you."

But then look what happened to the man who was given the smallest amount, or the smallest responsibility, and what did he do with it? Nothing . . . absolutely nothing! Did he get "promoted" because his first task was so menial he did nothing with it? Nope, what little he had was taken away from him and given to the one who had the most, and reread what the next sentence says about the abundance being given to the one who uses well what he is given, but pity the man who is unfaithful, because even what little responsibility he has shall be taken from him.

And it so specifically says to begin the "joyous" tasks. God wants to give each one of His abundant life so that we can say "Praise the Lord" and even "Praise the Lord Anyway" when the going is rough, but how can He give it to us when we are not obedient to Him? God's love is not conditional upon our works, and there's no question about that, but God's blessings and joy are abundantly bestowed on those who are obedient to Him.

Well, is it time for another conference with God? Just ask what's the first thing He wants you to do. And then let's go ahead and do it, and expect all kinds of miracles to happen because they will.

I just happened to look back at the opposite page of my Bible, and could hardly contain myself as two verses jumped out at me from the 24th chapter of Matthew, verses 46 and 47 (LNT). "Blessings on you if I return and find you faithfully doing your work. I will put such faithful ones in charge of everything I own!"

That's God's promise! Do we dare stand still just inside the door, or do we hurry to find all that He's got for us? I'm selfish, because I want everything that God's got for me, so come with me, will you? Let's find all the love and joy and peace and contentment that God has for those who love Him.

CHAPTER X

Praise the Lord—
For His Abiding Love!

THERE'S ALWAYS AN urgency as I write the last chapter of a book to be sure that nothing has been left out, and as I reread how God wants to work in and through us, I'm reminded we have to believe that "If any man be in Christ, he is a new creature: old things are passed away; behold, ALL things are become new." We've got to believe that Jesus Christ can rid us of our hangups, our old nature, our old griping disposition; we've got to believe that Jesus Christ can make a totally new creature out of us. We've got to believe that, even in the midst of the most adverse circumstances, God loves us, and because we are new creatures with a new nature this is possible.

But another thought just flashed through my mind. Maybe right now some are reading these pages and not understanding why their life has not been transformed or why they are not new creatures, in spite of having gone to church all their lives. Is Christ really in your heart? Have you ever made a real commitment to Him, and just simply asked Him to come into your heart and take over your life and make a new creature of you? If not, before you read this last chapter, why don't you do it?

About two and a half years before I met my beloved husband, he was aware that after attending church all of his life and fulfilling every position possible in the church, he was still not a "new" creature. How his life was transformed and the circumstances which could have led to great defeat became victorious are told in this chapter.

Charles had a tremendous burden to complete this before we were married, and he sent me one of the twenty copies he mailed out. I want to share it with you with a prayer that you will look beyond the human sorrows in this and discover how God made a new creature out of him through a series of remarkable circumstances. He has never put a title to it, so I have very simply called it

A TRIBUTE TO GOD
by Charles E. Hunter

What a mighty God we serve, when we really serve Him! This could be a sad story with a bitter ending, but because it is a relating of a series of real, living events God directed in every small detail, it is a story of many thrilling and joyful experiences in the lives of two people deeply in love with each other, but more deeply in love with our Lord Jesus Christ and our God.

Jeanne and I were married June 10, 1942, and experienced twenty-seven years of near perfect married life together before her death on May 23, 1969.

As I look at the two paragraphs above, they do not seem compatible, i.e., "joy" and "death." The fact that they have been very compatible in our lives is one of the miracles God really does when He is given freedom to control our lives fully.

Jeanne and I were Christians throughout our married life and before we met. We regularly attended church and served in just about every activity from participants to leaders in music, administration, and spiritual areas. We worked sincerely and hard in every responsibility we were given.

Churches all over the world depend on the thousands of Christians who do these services and this is the natural response of those desiring to do their best for God.

But this isn't all God wants from us. OUR BEST IS NOT GOOD ENOUGH.

In God's eyes "all our righteousnesses are as filthy rags" (Isaiah 64:6). God wants us just as we are, but He wants us to turn loose of ourselves and let Him do His work through us.

The greatest of all that happened to Jeanne and me was our doing this one simple, yet most important, act —"turning loose" of ourselves in full surrender of our lives to God.

Moses at age forty was one of the most qualified men in the history of the world to lead the children of Israel out of Egypt, but when he tried to do it his way, he utterly failed. After forty more years of waiting for God to tell him again to do his job, he said at age eighty that he was too old and feeble to do it and God said that was the way he wanted it so He, God, could lead the Israelites "through" Moses. Moses did exactly as God instructed him—he turned loose of himself and let God work through him.

Including time away from home for military service, Jeanne attended a small church in Houston, Texas, for forty years of her forty-five years on earth. My church "work" also lasted about forty years. In October 1967, we both felt very clearly God's will was for us to change to another place of worship. We had planned to change about five years sooner, but it seemed it was meant for us to wait.

We visited several churches and in January 1968, we attended a service at another church near our home. When we got home Jeanne said, "That's our church, isn't it?"; I readily agreed. We joined the choir within two or three weeks. We never knew why God led us to this change until late in Jeanne's life, but we knew it was part of His plan for our lives, and since then many of His reasons have been made abundantly clear.

During the four weeks preceding Easter, 1968, the

men of the church met at 6:45 A.M. each Wednesday for breakfast, devotion, and prayer at the church altar. This was a great inspiration to me to see about a hundred or more men kneeling before God to start their day. After Easter I found this to be a regular prayer group of eight to twelve men meeting for coffee and doughnuts before a devotional talk rotated among the men, and then prayer.

It was in about May 1968, at the altar one morning that I "turned loose" of my life and asked God to take full control. This I had come close to at times before, but never was quite willing to go all the way. Jeanne had developed tumors in her abdominal area which had grown quite large and she was facing surgery. We had no thought of cancer and felt that the only danger we had was the normal danger of something going wrong during the operation. This did not seem a big factor in my decision to turn my life fully over to God.

I recall in my prayer of asking God to take both Jeanne's and my life completely (spiritually) and if He wanted to take her or my life (physically) to do that, but at any cost to make us like He wanted us.

Nearly a year later, on a Saturday in late March, I read the 14th chapter of Luke four times and nothing would register. On Sunday morning I told myself I wouldn't attempt that chapter again and started reading the 15th chapter, but couldn't go beyond a few lines. The Holy Spirit seemed to say go back, so I did and although I had read this many times before, this time the 25th to the 35th verses said in God's words exactly what He expects if we want to be His Disciples—among other things it affirmed that I must put Christ as far above my love for Jeanne as love is above hate.

Jeanne's surgery on June 20, 1968, was, we thought a total success. By July 20 the doctor released her to go to Indiana with me; to climb mountains, swim, or anything she felt like. For four wonderful months, she had apparent perfect health.

About the middle of November, Jeanne started gaining weight rapidly and November 22, 1968, the doctor told her the sad and shocking news that the mass was growing and in response to her direct question, he said it was malignant. He told us after her June surgery that an ovary was malignant, but that he thought he had successfully removed the malignancy. This announcement in November, that it was growing again, frightened Jeanne, as it would anyone, and for two days she was constantly afraid. Saturday night about nine o'clock she asked me to call our pastor to pray for her. I called and talked to him three or four minutes and when I walked back in the bedroom, she said, "I'm not afraid any more," and she was never afraid again the rest of her life. This was another miracle in her life.

For three nights Jeanne knelt at the foot of our bed and fully committed her life to God. The next Tuesday our pastor visited us and Jeanne told him that *she was healed spiritually and that it wasn't important whether she was ever physically healed,* although she wanted to be. She talked to him about how perfect our love had been for our twenty-seven years of marriage and that we had been abundantly blessed, that she had received more happiness from this than most people who live many years longer.

I heard our pastor comment to others later, that whether Jeanne would ever be physically healed, she was already spiritually healed and this was all that really mattered.

One night a few weeks after Jeanne died, I was reading the Bible and when I came to 1 John 4:8 and read, "There is no fear in love, but perfect love casts out fear," I stopped reading and wrote the pastor a letter, expressing to him how their perfect love for Christ was so well demonstrated by this scripture because fear instantly left Jeanne when she had asked me to call him in November. She always was thrilled by his visits and never wanted to let him go.

On the morning of her birthday, after she had lost the use of her legs, she asked me to get someone to help me get her into the car. I called the church with the hopes of finding someone available. While I was speaking to one of the secretaries, the pastor knew in some way and intercepted the call. When I explained our need, he said, "Don't ask for one of my assistants when you need help—I want to be a part of this."

He came into her bedroom a few minutes later and as soon as she saw him, she said, "I didn't expect the General!" It was this marvelous Godly love between them that caused Jeanne to speak her last words on earth to our pastor as he left her bedside about three hours before her death. She simply said from her heart of love, "Don't go!"

One of the great changes in Jeanne, noticed by so many people, was the spirit of love she had for everyone with whom she came in contact. Her attitude was inspiring to everyone who visited her. People came to visit her often, dreading to face a friend with terminal cancer, but leaving with an uplifted spirit from the realization that her attitude was perfectly in tune with Christ. I don't remember anyone visiting her who didn't get a great blessing from it.

This love reached even beyond her direct contacts. On the afternoon of her death, a nurse stayed with us the last two or three hours and made the remark that her love found its way into the whole wing of the hospital, not just to the nurses attending her, but to patients she didn't even know.

Jeanne became weaker and spent most of the time in bed until she was hospitalized on December 31, 1968. As her strength waned, we called upon God many,

many times for physical strength and He always gave this quickly and just enough for our needs.

I recall one time in December we dressed her to go to the beauty parlor for a shampoo and set. She walked as far as a bench at our front door and almost collapsed. My knees hit the floor about as fast as she hit the bench and I asked God for strength. Immediately she stood up, walked to the car, made her trip to the beauty parlor and walked from the car back to her bed. I called these "little miracles" but they were mighty big in the assurance that God was with us every minute of the day and night in a very real way; and this is the way God wants to work in everything in a Christian's life and does when we let him. This is the work of the Holy Spirit when He controls.

On Monday, March 17, the doctor motioned for me to see him in the hospital corridor, after he examined Jeanne. The message he gave was very direct; he said, "Mrs. Hunter has three to six weeks to live—do you want me to tell her, so she can make her final arrangements?" I believed God would heal her and I replied to the doctor that she had already made her final arrangements spiritually (I thank God most of all for this) and that I would tell her. I never mentioned the time limitation to her, but did tell her the doctors had tried almost every medication known to them, with no results.

This caused me to feel that something had to be done quickly and I searched my mind and heart for a way to know what God expected of me. The next day I went home for about two hours and called several people of unusual faith for prayer for her healing. Wednesday I went to work for a few hours for a client of mine, a very sincere Christian who gave his life to the Lord, along with his wife, his son and daughter-in-law when in 1956 cancer was taking the life of his son. He had a great compassion for us and longed to help in any way possible.

84

It only took a few minutes with him for God's purpose in this visit to be revealed. He and his wife were personally acquainted with authors Agnes Sanford and Genevieve Parkhurst and when he asked if I would like for him to contact these ladies for prayer, my heart was thrilled beyond words and they placed the calls.

We had read *The Healing Light* by Agnes Sanford and *Healing and Wholeness Are Yours* by Genevieve Parkhurst and our faith had been deeply inspired to know that God was healing today through these ladies as He did through Christ when He was on earth. Although we believed in God's healing power and had heard of many instances of healings, we had not heard of such freedom as God's power through these two ladies.

I was rarely doing any work during this period and was with Jeanne almost constantly night and day, but God had a reason for me to go to this particular office at this particular time. He could have made these arrangements at any time, but it was His plan for Jeanne's condition to reach a point beyond the help of the finest known medical aid available, then he moved in this wonderful, swift way. It's really thrilling!

On Thursday night while I was out of Jeanne's hospital room for about ten minutes, Edith Drury called Jeanne from California. She had worked for years with Agnes Sanford, and God has used her in many instances of healing. Jeanne loved *The Healing Light* and probably spent more time early in 1969 reading this than any other book. This was one way the Holy Spirit had of building Jeanne's trust in God and Christ. It was only a normal and natural response after the Holy Spirit had prepared Jeanne's mind and heart, for her to receive such a tremendous inspiration when Edith Drury called.

After talking with Jeanne a few minutes, she said she, in prayer, would be holding Jeanne before Christ and in her mind's eye, as a lady forty-five years of age, in perfect health, singing in the choir and working in the church; she asked Jeanne to do the same and to fix her eyes on Jesus and take them off herself. Jeanne really, with all her heart, tried to do this and it was most difficult, because her abdomen was almost twice its normal size; but I'm sure that this continuing prayer was one of the richest experiences of her life.

One of Jeanne's favorite choruses became very meaningful at this time, and I can recall one night in the hospital while four friends were visiting, they had just finished prayer for her and she started singing, as all of us joined her:

Turn your eyes upon Jesus,
Look full in His wonderful face
And the things of this earth
Will grow strangely dim
In the light of His glory and grace.

Friday night at 7:30 Genevieve Parkhurst called, she talked to me a few minutes and then to Jeanne. She said she would send us her latest book, *Healing the Whole Person,* which was recently released; that she would be praying for Jeanne and would be back in touch.

Back in November, just after Jeanne was told the malignancy existed, a friend brought us her book *Healing and Wholeness Are Yours.* As Jeanne and I read this and the many promises in the New Testament, we believed that Jeanne would be healed physically. At this time God planted in her mind something far greater than physical healing because she was given such absolute assurance, that already she had all the healing needed, because God had completely healed her SPIRITUALLY.

I never realized until after her death that this was the greatest faith I had ever witnessed—yet it seemed so simple. My heart leaps with joy when I think how beautifully and peacefully this marvelous acceptance of the perfect will of God sustained such a tremendous attitude in her through the last six months of her life; six months which could have been to both of us a nightmare of sorrow and horror, but which was really the happiest period of our lives.

It seemed a long time from Friday night till the next Tuesday (March 25, 1969) when at noon Genevieve Parkhurst's book *Healing the Whole Person* arrived in the hospital. Jeanne's strength was waning rapidly; she had hardly slept Monday night and Tuesday all day she was restless, couldn't go to sleep even with shots which always made her sleep and she said she felt like climbing the walls. This was unusual, for her. Eight days of the three to six weeks the doctor had estimated were gone and they were too rapidly showing how right he was.

I didn't leave the hospital room all that day. I read all afternoon in the book, in very deep meditation and prayer, and by seven-thirty that evening had only read twenty-nine pages, but Christ was really close. At seven-thirty Mrs. Parkhurst called and I guess because I was relying so much on her prayers, it was the most welcome call of my life. She talked to me a few minutes and then to Jeanne. When she started talking, Jeanne's mind and voice cleared instantly from the dullness of medication they were giving her for tenseness.

She was so weak that she was able to sit up only by holding my arm to pull her up; she could not stand at all during the past week. You could tell, by her response, how very thrilled she was to be talking and listening to Mrs. Parkhurst, and I was elated. They finished talking about seven-forty; Jeanne lay back down and I started reading again in the book; Mrs. Parkhurst told me later that she started praying for Jeanne and must have prayed till about eight o'clock.

Within five minutes Jeanne was asleep and slept twelve hours, which was longer than anytime she had slept in the twenty-seven years we were married. And then, the tremendous power of God visited that hospital room through the night and that became the most memorable night of my life.

At eight o'clock I was reading in the quietness of the room with my mind all on Christ while Jeanne slept, but then I was startled by a voice so clear and strong that for an instant I thought a man was in the room and spoke.

The voice spoke only three words, but what marvelous words they were: "JEANNE IS HEALED!" I was exuberantly, profoundly filled with the greatest joy I had ever known! For almost six months, I had believed with all my heart that Jeanne *would be* healed, but after doing everything I knew to do, praying with all the sincerity I could muster, reading the Bible probably over a thousand hours, seeking to know how to find faith as big as a grain of mustard seed, meditating on the many very clear and simple promises of the Bible, I had reached the exact point from which I started six months before—only with a belief; really not faith, that Jeanne *would be* healed, which was exactly nothing.

Faith is knowing with absolute certainty that what is not visibly so, actually is so. I was shown in a very clear and simple way that until I reached absolute zero in my power, until I became nothing, until I became totally helpless before God, He could also do nothing for me.

It took Moses forty years herding sheep to reach this point. Jeanne and I had spent forty years believing we could really do good work for God as long as He was available to help us when we needed Him. Well, we really needed Him now, but we needed more than His help—we needed His power. And He abundantly gave it; more than we could ever dream or imagine; but He didn't *help* us—*He did it all himself.* He no longer

88

needed to be available to help us; we needed only to be totally available for Him to work through us as His human channel.

Every time I think of the voice of Christ actually audibly speaking to me personally, it is an awesome feeling to finally realize that God and Christ are not back in history with Moses, or Abraham, or David, or Elijah—and they are not just off somewhere in space or beyond space—that they are not just in Heaven waiting till we get there, so they can greet us; they, through their Holy Spirit, are *living* within us, if we have salvation, and they can only become active in us when we reach a complete state of vacuum, so far as our own righteousness or power is concerned, and we turn loose of everything and let them tell us what to do!

When God and Christ do what they say in their promises, they really do it right! Just those three words, spoken audibly by the same Jesus Christ our Lord who spoke to Saul on the road to Damascus, changed my life in an instant, just as surely as He changed Saul into Paul, and I say "Paul" with the full meaning that reveals God's total accomplishments through him. It humbles me to realize that this actually happened to me. But they were not through doing great things that night.

I went to bed at 10:30 P.M. and with thanks to God for healing Jeanne my only prayer, I dropped asleep. My whole life for six months had been centered around Jeanne's healing and now I was sure it had been accomplished. About three o'clock as I lay awake and in meditation and joyful thanks to God, I had another experience which I'm sure I shall never forget.

I presume what happened was a vision, but a vision alive with feeling. I first saw my body about eighteen inches above my physical body and it started rising—then I saw Mrs. Parkhurst, whom I had never met except by phone, with her hands under my back lifting me until I was as high as she could reach and then I kept rising higher and higher. From the time the vision started, a series of impulses somewhat like soundwaves were flowing through my whole body; they grew stronger and more rapid the higher I went, and I have no idea how high that was.

Apparently what was happening was Mrs. Parkhurst, through her close communion with Christ, was lifting me in prayer before Christ, and this was a most fantastic experience. I didn't see Christ, but I felt Him very plainly. After being held at this height a moment, I began to descend and so did the waves of impulses begin to lessen, until the heavenly experience ended as it started—and it was marvelous.

Even these two appearances of Christ in my life didn't add up to the hundredfold of blessings He promised if we would become His disciples in total surrender, so within about an hour, He showered His tremendous love again.

All during Jeanne's illness, since about November, as we grew more and more dependent upon God and daily submitted our lives more deeply to Him, we found He quickly answered our prayers for what we called little miracles—the big one was for her healing. As I lay on my hospital cot, excited and thrilled about the two experiences God had given me, I watched Jeanne as she slept. Because of the medication she was taking, her mouth was very dry and I could see her trying to find just a little moisture.

Remember how the children of Israel sought water in the wilderness and found it only when Moses, in obedience to God, struck the rock (Christ), with his rod and water was supplied? And remember that the water Christ promised was the kind which stopped your thirst forever?

I asked God, just as we had asked so many times for little miracles and received them, to please relieve her of this dryness. In very distinct words, although not audible, the Holy Spirit said, "Charles, let Me do this My way." In a few minutes I asked for something else and again he said, "Charles, let Me do this My way"; a few minutes later when I asked still another time for something he said again, "Charles, let Me do this My way." I finally got the message, and after this, I could never again pray for anything specific for Jeanne, but always prayed that He would do everything He planned "His way."

I didn't fully realize that this was not just His instructions for His way of caring for Jeanne, but that He was instructing me to let Him direct every event of my life "His way." What a fantastic night this was!

Jeanne wondered why these miracles were not directed to her instead of me. Perhaps it was because God had healed her spiritually "His way" and it was I who needed a heavenly balm, to heal me in preparation for His service.

The following Saturday, when the doctor came to examine Jeanne, she said, "Why don't you let me go home on pass during the day and I'll come back at night?" He replied, "Why not," so for five days we left the hospital after she was examined and returned about six o'clock in the evening. She gained strength sufficient to sit up for an hour or more at a time, sat in the sunshine and even played her organ, foot pedals and all! We were very excited about her marvelous progress and knew it all started when Christ said, "Jeanne is healed!"

After these thrilling, joyful five days, the doctors kept her in the hospital three days for transfusions and observation. The next day, April 6, was Easter and Jeanne spent the day at home and it was not a day of beautiful sunshine outside, where she stayed an hour and a half, but the sunshine in our thankful hearts was brighter still inside.

Then, on the morning of the fourth day, I knew with excitement, two hours before the doctors arrived, what was going to happen, and it did! The doctor examined her and with words I'm sure even thrilled him like it did us, he said, "Mrs. Hunter, how would you like to be dismissed and come back once a week, as an out-patient?"

Although they never said so, I feel sure that back on March 17 the doctors never expected her to get out of her hospital bed alive. She walked very well to the living room and dinette during the day, and sat up quite a long time, enjoyed more strength than she had for many weeks, and stood for her first shower bath in a long time. Her strength continued to improve and our thrilling joy increased until about April 22, when she had a high fever and an infection. This put her back in bed and quickly took the strength from her legs. This continued through the rest of the week.

Saturday night, Genevieve Parkhurst called and without saying hello, asked how Jeanne was. I said, "Not good," and she said, "I know it—God says that I must go to Houston to see Jeanne." She said she was booked heavily and didn't know how she could find the time, but God would do it and for me to stand by till she knew. The next Monday was April 28, Jeanne's forty-fifth birthday, and her day to go for her out-patient treatment. Except for the loss of strength in her legs, she felt good. The doctor said he liked her blood count and felt the weakness was temporary. The only time in her illness Jeanne ever pleaded for anything was that she wanted her legs back. She never received an answer to this pleading.

The next Thursday night, Genevieve Parkhurst called and said, "Meet the plane at 1:05 Friday" (May 2). She stayed in our home until Sunday morning. I felt the very presence of Christ through her sensitive relationship to Him. These two days with Mrs. Parkhurst were

92

filled with her love and prayers for Jeanne and in her talking with us about the marvels of the power of Christ. I felt I was sitting at the feet of a saint, drinking in the glories of what a real live God had meant to her in her total surrender to His perfect will.

Apparently the Holy Spirit used her to prepare Jeanne and me for the final events of our physical lives together. Certainly we were completely prepared—not with strength or wisdom of our own, but with our attitudes healed and healthy—ready, willing, and actually anxious for His great and mighty loving power to usher her into the eternity He describes as a mansion prepared in heaven—a home especially built for those who serve Him.

No apparent physical change came to Jeanne from the personal visit of Mrs. Parkhurst and it is clear now that God was concerned with spiritual healing. He even displayed the abundance of His personal concern for us by giving Jeanne this short period of physical healing to assure her and me that, when we pray, if we have faith even the size of a grain of mustard seed, He hears and answers—"His way."

He gave us this beautiful answer to our many months of knocking, searching, and seeking in physically moving her from her hospital bed to the home she loved and in showing us with absolute certainty that He heard our prayer for physical healing, but that He had something much greater for both of us.

It is beautiful how God chose Genevieve Parkhurst to be His instrument in our spiritual healings from the first week of our knowledge of cancer (her book *Healing and Wholeness Are Yours*); then at the very door of death, to bring her back into our lives with her perfect faith to be a channel for His power to heal body, mind, and spirit, as she so well describes in her book *Healing the Whole Person*, and finally about an hour after Jeanne's death by a phone call, followed later by a letter, which explained Jeanne's anxiety during the period between Mrs. Parkhurst's visit in our home and Jeanne's death, to go on into eternity and to her perfect healing in heaven.

Jeanne begged me during her last two or three weeks to turn her loose and let her die. This was not a despondent plea for death, but an indescribable plea to let her go to her God she learned to know so perfectly and personally that she had complete confidence in His promises. She had once remarked that I would never give up in my quest for her healing and she constantly referred to me as her lifeline, so much so that during her last three months she would not be satisfied for even a short period of my absence, even with her mother, whom she deeply loved, with her. One thing I know, she had from me the most complete love possible from a human and her love for me was equally as strong.

Here is an extract from a letter dated June 19 from Mrs. Parkhurst:

"I agree with you that so far as God was concerned, Jeanne was healed in the hospital when you were told this—but Jeanne's heart was not in this world—she saw a city built by God in the Heavens, and the pull of that glorious place was too much for the things of earth to overcome. She wanted to go on. So we shall not regret her going, but rejoice and be glad that God has prepared a place for her that is so lovely this earth could not hold her."

Now, let me repeat some verses from the Phillips translation of the New Testament,* which so perfectly shows how the Holy Spirit of God and Christ speaks to us, as He spoke through the Word of God to me, after I received Mrs. Parkhurst's letter: "All these whom we have mentioned (Abel, Enoch, Noah, Abraham and

---

*The New Testament in Modern English, by J. B. Phillips, New York, The Macmillan Company.

Sarah) maintained their faith, but died without receiving God's promises, tho they had seen them in the distance, had hailed them as true and were quite convinced of their reality. They freely admitted that they lived on this earth as exiles and foreigners. Men who say that mean, of course, that their eyes are fixed upon their true homeland. If they had meant the particular country they had left behind, they had ample opportunity to return.

"No, the fact is that they longed for a better country altogether, nothing less than a heavenly one. And because of this faith of theirs, God is not ashamed to be called their God, for in sober truth, he has prepared for them a city" (Hebrews 11:13–16).

Then in Hebrews 11, about Enoch, he said, "The man who approaches God must have faith in two things, first that God exists and secondly that it is worth a man's while to try to find God." And it truly is! Then, in another place, Christ said, "If you knew where I was going, you would be glad." In Romans 8:14, he said, "You have been adopted into the very family circle of God and you can say with a full heart, 'Father, my Father.' " The Spirit himself endorses our inward conviction that we really are the children of God.

"Think what that means. If we are his children, we share his treasures and all that Christ claims as His will belong to all of us as well! Yes, if we share in His sufferings, we shall certainly share in his glory."

And Jeanne is sharing now in his marvelous glory— the ultimate goal of anyone who truly loves God. Just as an added assurance to me that she reached that goal, following her death at seven o'clock in the evening, after I had gone to bed and relaxed in God's love, really happy and secure in the knowledge that God had done everything "His way," I saw in Heaven a choir of angels singing and the Holy Spirit let me know that Jeanne was among them also, really happy and secure.

Particularly the last six months of her life, although her health had rapidly waned and extreme weakness, fatigue, and fever plagued her, she attained a faith in God far greater than any I have ever seen, and approached eternity with such an eager, positive assurance that there was absolutely no room for doubt that she was personally, literally a child of God going to her eternal home joyfully.

I thank God with all my heart for not only answering the prayer I made at the altar of our church about a year before her death, but for answering it "His way." He promised if we trusted Him He would give us more than we could ever dream or imagine, and He did! He gave His profound answer to my prayer in completely taking both of our lives spiritually, and her life physically, because he wanted to, and at the cost Jeanne and I were fully willing to pay.

During the last days of her life, at her death and for the past six months since then, I have been so completely loved by God that He placed a shield around me to prevent any loneliness, sadness, grief, or depression whatever, except for twenty minutes in Anderson, Indiana, two months after her death. I had started my audit of the college records that morning. At five o'clock that afternoon, I left the college alone to go for a sandwich. The most horrible, lonely, heavy, dark, grief-stricken period I had ever experienced came upon me and, by the time my sandwich came I had tears all the way into my heart and felt I could stand it no longer. I cried out, "Lord take it away!" Instantly all signs and feelings of depression left and I was completely, jubilantly happy, and since then, not one sign of loneliness or grief has visited me. What a mighty God we serve!

The Lord giveth, the Lord taketh away—Blessed be the name of the Lord.